BUSINESS PERFORMANCE

Process & Techniques for Building a Lean Enterprise for Business.

Ross Pypkin

Table of Contents

INTRODUCTION

Many of the world's best start-ups which are innovative, face overwhelming challenges right out of the door. As indicated by Forbes, about 90% of businesses will come up short. Let that hit home for a moment. The vast majority of new companies will fall flat! That is a reality, so sober in nature, for business entrepreneurs when they are putting time and cash into a business that is quite new. The truth of the matter is, new business start-ups need a chilly, hard portion of reality when thinking about entering the domain of fierce business competition. Why those strong business start-ups keep on bouncing into the fire, regardless of these realities, is challenging. A business person flourishes with difficulties, and it drives them to conquer such resistance and battle to win. This business environment competitive in nature, requires an entrepreneur to work more enthusiastically, more intelligent and utilize each conceivable competitive edge to endure. The Lean Six Sigma is that upper hand for business people to get dexterous, and inevitably effective.

Lean Six Sigma gives a thorough and organized way to provide the necessary assistance and improve quality and performance, and to take care of possibly complex issues. It encourages you to utilize the correct devices, in a place that is right and in the correct way, as well as in your everyday administration. Lean Six Sigma truly is tied in with getting key standards and ideas into the DNA and backbone of your business so it turns into a characteristic piece of how you get things done.

This book looks to support business managers and leaders to better comprehend their job role and improve hierarchical proficiency and effectiveness. You might want to have results change. With this, you have to understand that results or outcomes are the consequence of frameworks. It is the framework or manner in which individuals cooperate, work together and connect. Furthermore, these frameworks are the result of how individuals think and carry on. Along these lines, if you have the need to change results, you need to change your frameworks, and to do that, you need to change your reasoning.

The thoughts about Lean Six Sigma isn't about resource stripping and 'making do'. Rather, this methodology centers around doing the correct things right, with the goal that you truly include an incentive for the client and make your business compelling and productive. The fundamental focal point of the book identifies with DMAIC (Define, Measure, Analyze, Improve and Control). This is the Lean Six Sigma technique for improving existing procedures that form part of the business system or frameworks, and it gives a perfect method to help you in your search for constant improvement. At the point when you have to build up another procedure, the Design for Six Sigma technique becomes possibly the most important factor. Known as DMADV (Define, Measure, Analyze, Design and Verify).

Beginning a business can be an alarming — however exciting — process. Such huge numbers of things can determine if your start-up will succeed or come up short. The Lean Six Sigma is a way of thinking in business that have spotlights on accomplishing more with less. This implies extending resources to the most extreme while downplaying costs. With the Lean Six Sigma strategies, you'll discover building your business is not so much frightening but rather more exciting than at any other time. Start-ups, Small and Medium Scaled organizations (SMEs) should constantly improve or have risk of dying off. A quality program is basic to guarantee sustainability through time, yet not all business people know about the relevance of applying quality management techniques to independent ventures, with the vast majority of them believing it's just for huge organizations. A smaller organization may not understand the colossal returns of a huge organization, yet that doesn't diminish the effect of a quality program's investment returns. Quality is critical to consumer satisfaction in any business. It is all the more so for new businesses as they are yet to set up themselves in the market. Quality in its least complex structure is characterized as meeting the desires for the client. Six sigma reasoning gives the devices to accomplish this goal.

The desires for the client will constantly change as new items with better features, improved assistance quality, lower cost items with features that are similar, become accessible from competitors. Thus, constant improvement is vital to keep clients.

The issue is that everyday tasks regularly redirect the business proprietor's consideration based on what is useful for the organization in the long haul, permitting just a little amount of time (assuming any) to arranging and forestalling issues. Six Sigma is one of the quality techniques few in nature, that

can be applied from the earliest starting point, and could bring about high investment funds, particularly in business that produce a high volume of standard items or administrations consistently.

Distinguishing the components behind the success of a business comes down to research and experience. Research may incorporate perusing business books and online journals, going to workshops, and talking with seasoned and well prepared businessmen. The experience may incorporate figuring out speculative plans to concoct real answers. Lamentably, in this research and confirmation, one factor seldom gets talked about or investigated: the skill of critical thinking and problem solving. This is a disturbing oversight since having success in business depends on your capacities to take care of issues when they emerge. Luckily, the Lean methodology will rapidly raise you to an acceptable level on the best way to take care of your most serious issues. Creating critical thinking and problem solving skills will make it far simpler to accomplish your objectives by limiting expenses and maximizing profits. With this in place, you'll additionally convey higher worth, amuse clients, and quickly develop your business.

In the midst of emergency, markets, organizations, and strategies rapidly evolve; the competitive scene changes and new buyer patterns rise. In such occasions, the business choices can seal their destiny: do close to nothing and join the positions of others in the battle to hold piece of the overall industry and decreasing margins, or do something transformational and rise considerably more grounded than previously—best ready to outperform the competition once the market recover and request resurges. Businesses must create close term systems to endure the downturn, and longer-term procedures to flourish in the new economy. This book gives a down to earth comprehension of how Lean Six Sigma (LSS) underpins both the close term need to survive by securely and quickly decreasing expense, and the more drawn out term direction to a good performance by developing into a quick and spry business enterprise. And keeping in mind that consistent procedure improvement is regularly connected with continuous, steady performance gains, this book shows how a purposeful spotlight on procedure and execution can empower a basic, operational, and cultural change that gives a good competitive advantage.

All through the book, there is the urge to continue asking yourself how and for what reason things are done. What's the motivation behind your items and services and also the processes that give them support? In a perfect world, things are done so as to meet the prerequisites of your clients, yet you have to know what their identity is, or who they may be. This part centers around recognizing your different, and very unique, clients, perceiving how you can decide their necessities, and telling the best way to utilize this information to shape the premise of the estimation set for your procedures. In doing such, you have to investigate some procedure processes, as well. By drawing a present state or 'as is' business process map, you can perceive what the procedure truly resembles and get a comprehension on who does what, when, where and why. Generally, you're building up an image of your clients and the business process that look to meet what they need.

Another business person can contend at the levels by conveying a logical Lean Six Sigma program. Having a sense of differentiation by using a strong Six Sigma methodology will give noteworthy standing with organizations in competition. Grasping this system of persistent improvement makes a domain for an innovation to bloom. Supporting and empowering that development pushes a startup forward, without extending resources excessively far.

Lean Six Sigma systems that are appropriately actualized will fuel advancement, balance resource allotment, and maintain an attention on nonstop quality improvement. Finding that parity and staying coordinated in a consistently changing condition will keep an inventive startup out of that 90% fragment that falls flat.

CHAPTER ONE:
THE BASICS OF LEAN SIX SIGMA

Lean Six Sigma is a strategy that depends on team collaboration to improve performance by expelling waste in a systematic manner and diminishing variation. It consolidates lean manufacturing/lean enterprise and Six Sigma to dispose of the eight sorts of waste (muda): Defects, Over-Production, Waiting, Non-Utilized Talent, Transportation, Inventory, Motion, and Extra-Processing.

Lean Six Sigma lessens process imperfections and waste, yet in addition gives a structure to general organizational culture change. By presenting Lean Six Sigma, the outlook of employees and directors change to one that spotlights on development and ceaseless improvement through process advancement. This adjustment in culture and the outlook of a business boosts effectiveness and expands productivity.

Six Sigma tries to improve the nature of procedure yields by distinguishing and expelling the reasons for defects (errors) and limiting changeability in business forms. Together, Lean intends to accomplish ceaseless flow by fixing the linkages between process steps while Six Sigma centers around diminishing procedure variety (in the entirety of its structures) for the process steps which enables a fixing of those linkages. To put it plainly, Lean uncovered wellsprings of process variety and Six Sigma intends to lessen that variety empowering a virtuous pattern of iterative upgrades towards the objective of persistent flow.

Lean Six Sigma utilizes the DMAIC stages like that of Six Sigma. The five stages incorporate Define, Measure, Analyze, Improve, and Control. The five stages utilized in Lean Six Sigma are expected to recognize the underlying driver of wasteful aspects and works with any process, product or service that has a lot of information or quantifiable qualities available. The DMAIC toolbox of Lean Six Sigma includes all the Lean and Six Sigma tools.

The satisfaction of the consumer is of topmost priority in any business. Consumer satisfaction additionally implies profitability. Any business success relies upon the capacity to guarantee the highest quality at the most reduced expense. During the 1980s when most organizations accepted that creating quality items was excessively expensive, Motorola accepted the inverse: "the better, the less expensive." It understood that by delivering a product of high quality, the expense of production goes down. Motorola realized that more prominent consumer satisfaction produces higher profitability. Today, market competition leaves no space for mistake. It is currently important to implement the ideas of Lean Six Sigma. Lean Six Sigma is a business methodology wherein the focus is to improve the primary concern and increase consumer satisfaction.

The blend of these two incredible assets, Lean and Six Sigma system, will bring about business process variation reduction and dramatic bottom line (language of CEO) improvement. Since all organizations are in the matter of accomplishing quicker profit on investments, especially for their investors, utilizing Lean standards in Six Sigma is critical. For the business architecting Six Sigma theory in its foundation, Lean velocity can quicken the usage and benefits of the business process.

Lean Six Sigma is a procedure improvement strategy intended to take out issues, evacuate waste and wastefulness, and improve working conditions to give a better reaction to clients' needs. It joins the apparatuses, strategies and standards of Lean and Six Sigma into one popular and ground-breaking technique for improving your business tasks. Lean Six Sigma's team oriented methodology has demonstrated results in expanding productivity and significantly improving gainfulness for organizations around the globe.

LEAN AS A CONCEPT

The principal driver of Lean is the disposal of waste. A good portrayal of the Lean methodology is, "a lot of tools or techniques that aid the identitfication and the relentless disposal of waste." Let's assume a business is doing huge scale, high-amount generation like Toyota; at that point a process with some sort of waste in it implies that organization is making large scale, high amount waste. No organization wants to do this. The Lean methodology utilizes techniques to study the business process.

WASTE AND LEAN METHODOLOGY

The Lean philosophy recognizes and endeavors to remove waste of different sorts in business. Waste is something besides the normal measure of hardware, materials, parts, space, and workers time, which are significant to increase the value of the item.

Various kinds of waste have been characterized:

- Defects: An item that is announced unfit for use is a defect. This requires the item to either be rejected or reworked, costing the organization time and cash. Example can be seen in an item that is scratched during the generation process and assembly of an item in an incorrect manner because of indistinct instruction.

- Over-Production: This refers to a product that is made in abundance or made before it is required. Items ought to be created as they are required after the "Just-in-time" theory in Lean. Such an example is making pointless reports and overproduction of an item before a client has mentioned it. Perhaps you make more products because there is some extra crude material accessible or 30 minutes remaining on the shift. Or then again, you may make various adaptations of an item since you are not exactly sure what the client will purchase or how much. You may make more than you might suspect you need since you dread that a portion of the item may be faulty. Or on the other hand, you make 15 duplicates of a report for a gathering of which 13 individuals have agreed they will visit, just in the event that two additional individuals really appear. This concept of overproduction causes wastage of time and money, keeping both of those assets from being utilized for something different. Furthermore, this sort of waste can never be recovered.

- Waiting: Waiting includes delays in process steps and this is divided into two unique classes: laying wait for materials. Various examples include; waiting for approval from someone superior, waiting for an email reaction, for material conveyance, and slow or defective equipments. An administrator comes up short on crude material and needs to renew the stock. Or on the other hand, possibly the stock had been replenished yet, the material conveyed was damaged.

At the point when one machine is utilized to make various items, it might set aside effort to make the changeover starting with one occupation then onto the next. In an office, the approval to order material might leave the purchasing agent waiting, or a Human Resource agent needs to request extra information a job seeker before preparing the application.

- Non-Utilized Talent: This refers to the misuse of human potential and skill and is the most current addition. The primary driver of this waste is when the executives is isolated from workers. At the point when this happens, employees are not allowed the chance to give criticism and suggestions to administrators so as to improve the flow of business process and at such, it suffers. Examples can be; ineffectively prepared workers, absence of motivating forces for employees, and setting them in employments or places that don't use the entirety of their insight or skill.

- Transportation: Transportation is the pointless or inordinate movement of materials, item, individuals, gear, and tools. Transportation decreases the value of the item and can a form of damage or defect to such product or items. Examples include; moving item between various functional areas and sending overloaded stock back to an outlet distribution center. It can involve trucking material starting with one city then onto the next or having it shipped over the sea to carry out the subsequent stage of an operation. In an office environment, an individual may need to walk a long distance to obtain the output from the focal printer or walk up to duplicate a report.

- Inventory: This is an abundance of items and materials that aren't processed yet. This is an issue due to the fact that the item may get old before the client requires it, putting away the stock can cost the organization time and cash, and the probability of harm and defects can increase after some time. Examples include; finished goods in excess, completed products that can't be sold. This sort of stock can be the consequence of overproduction for any of the reasons recorded in that section. An inventory (excess inventory) created intentionally, to counter known or potential quality problems is called safety stock. What's more, stock waste isn't limited to manufacturing activities.

Numerous workplaces have stacks of paper beside every copier that will take a very long time to use; less paper at every copier would consume less space and would tie up less cash.

- Motion: Motion is superfluous individual movement. Motion in excessive manner waste time and increase the opportunity of damage. This can be; strolling to get equipment, reaching materials, and strolling to various parts of where goods are produced to finish various undertakings. This could include laborers involved in production, lifting heavy items from the floor to a table or transport line. It could be office laborers flexing muscles or bending to get something in their work area. Or then again it could be strolling to another structure that houses focal supplies so as to get a something. These examples remove laborers from work of great value and some of the time involve a wellbeing or health hazard. And keeping in mind that these examples may appear little, even miniscule, proportions of waste, they do add up. In the event that each individual in the business spends as meager as five minutes per day on these sorts of "built in" wasted movements, that means 25 minutes out of each week, which is over 20 hours out of every year per laborer.

- Extra-Processing: Extra-handling is accomplishing more work than is required or important to finish an assignment. Examples include; double entering data, pointless production steps, superfluous item customization, and utilizing higher accuracy gear than would normally be appropriate.

These wastes are not really autonomous. Creation of safety stock, without anyone else's input, is overproduction. If it is produced due to defect problems, that overproduction is additionally attached to the misuse of correction and stock waste. Or on the other hand consider the case of somebody who strolls to a focal printer to recover a report. There is wasted movement in getting up. What's more, there is movement waste in strolling from the printer to the workplace conveying the report. Does strolling from the workplace to the printer establish movement waste or transport waste? While a few people would invest energy discussing the issue (an exercise in futility in itself), most importantly it doesn't make a difference! For whatever length of time that the waste is recognized, the key is to figure out how to eliminate it. As you can most likely tell from both of these rundowns, the standards of Lean can be applied to any business procedure or activity, not simply producing. It is currently utilized in most capacities and businesses.

PRINCIPLES OF LEAN

Five principles of lean

Value

Value is dictated by what the client considers to be significant within an item or service, instead of what the people creating or conveying the item or service think. Numerous businesses neglect to see an item from the client's perspective. Items ought to be made to suit clients' needs; for instance, businesses may need to reconsider the item itself if request is poor as opposed to changing the marketing strategy. Basically, while making an item, ensure that you are tending to clients' needs and giving them what they need.

Value Stream

Business activities and steps associated with making and conveying items and services to the client; it is the connection of the steps together instead of thinking about each progression in an isolating manner. The value stream at the end of the day is the whole lifecycle of an item from the root of the crude material/plan to the completed item. In the event that a business inspects the whole procedure, it will quite often uncover a lot of waste (this is known as procedure re-designing). In the event that an association wishes to turn out to be genuinely lean, the worth stream must be broken down and improved.

Flow

This infer how much there is smooth continuous progression of activities that increase the value of the client, as opposed to waste and ineffectiveness that blocks the move through the value stream. For the incentive to flow, waste should be done away with. In a situation where the procedure neglects to push ahead, at that point this can be viewed as waste. A value stream should be made where each part of production is totally synchronized with the various components. A legitimate structure, along these lines, should be set up to ensure that the whole stream of production flow effectively, in this way disposing of waste.

Pull

This is how much the value stream is preparing items and services for which there is a client request, instead of making something and having hope somebody needs it. Instead of promoting the item to the client, you permit the client to pull the item from you. This approach guarantees that nothing is made early and encourages a substantially more synchronized flow. To accomplish this, more prominent adaptability is required just as an exceptionally short pattern of plan and generation.

Perfection

The persistent appraisal of significant value stream execution to distinguish and improve the value made and conveyed to the client, as opposed to resisting changes that improve the way toward making and conveying client value. An organization that is "going for lean" is taking a stab at flawlessness; in any case, this is a continuous process. A system making value to flow in a faster means will consistently uncover shrouded waste that is seen in the value stream. What becomes clear is that there is no closure to the way toward decreasing all the elements of waste, for example, time, cost and slip-ups. The organization should consistently make progress toward perfection.

CHAPTER TWO:
WHAT IS SIX SIGMA?

The Six Sigma approach is an archive of different demonstrated quality standards and strategies. Six Sigma drives a business toward the objective of finding the most minimal expense for the degree of value required, with quality being defined by the client. A new company should be a "lean enterprise".

Six Sigma is a critical thinking and problem solving system that decreases costs and improves the satisfaction of consumer by enormously lessening waste in all the processes associated with the creation and conveyance of products or items and additionally services. All the more explicitly, Six Sigma is a critical thinking and problem solving innovation that utilizations information, estimations, and statistics to distinguish the important elements that will drastically reduce waste and defects while expanding unsurprising outcomes, consumer satisfaction, profit and investor value.

Six Sigma was first created at Motorola during the late 1980s. The approach was spearheaded by Bill Smith, a quality engineer, whose objective was to improve the manner in which the quality and measurement frameworks worked in order to dispose of errors. The Motorola frameworks endured mistake rates that made an excessive amount of scrap, revamp, repetitive testing and regularly client disappointment.

The Six Sigma approach concentrated on distinguishing and disposing of whatever that cause variation in the process. At the point when the variety is gone, the process results can be definitely predicted – inevitably. By structuring the framework so these accurately unsurprising outcomes fall inside the zone of satisfactory execution from a client point of view, process mistakes are wiped out. Yet, the engineers at Motorola went above and beyond. They knew for a fact that many process changes were not compelling on the grounds that they didn't find a root cause for the problem. Likewise, the progressions they made would not stick, as the operators returned to getting things done in the first way after some time. Six Sigma was composed with five stages to address these issues.

In particular, accomplishing Six Sigma implies that close to 3.4 defects happen per one million "openings" to make an adequate yield. The name itself is the factual measure that portrays the defect rate. In this way, Six Sigma alludes to six standard deviations between the mean of a process and the specification for whatever yield is being estimated. Such specifications are dictated by clients.

The objective of the Six Sigma (6σ) procedure is a means of defect free process. The sigma level demonstrates the degree to which the business goes along towards having an defect free

process. Accomplishing a 6 sigma level truly implies: you commit an error just 3.4 occasions out of a million. (for example out of a million invoices, you just need to send 3 credit invoice).

WHY YOU NEED SIX SIGMA?

Does your business have issues? Do your business and activities forms encapsulate variations within? Your response will definitely be a reverberating YES! Numerous organizations have various adaptations of same chronic issues. The voices of the internal as well as external customers should be listened to and this regularly turns out to be clear. You may hear phrases like, "This is like the (X) issue we had on the (Y) program" or "Client B is encountering a similar interface issues with our framework as Customer A did a year ago" or "We've just gained a ton of ground on this issue." These sorts of expressions are demonstrative of systemic problems. Besides, how often has your business as far as anyone knows fixed, or endeavored to fix, these issues? Two extraordinary models are returns and remittances and abundance/outdated stock. How would we fix these issues? We apportion stores to cover the foreseen costs, yet does that ever fix the issue?

The answers for these sorts of ceaseless or fundamental issues are obscure to your business. This isn't as intense a supposition as one would at first assume, as it appears to be natural that in the event that you had the solutions, you would have just executed them. In this manner, regardless of whether the problems are old or fresh out of the box new, the variety is obscure, the underlying drivers of variety are unexplainable, and the lasting solutions are obscure. Current thinking brings current issues and isn't adequate to provide solutions to them. A few businesses truly accept that this variety is dark enchantment or a fine art, yet actually it isn't.

This is in remembrance to a huge advertising office that was visited which accepted that Six Sigma was not appropriate to its condition since it didn't have business forms like others; it offered 100 percent innovative types of assistance to its customers. This is additionally a recognizable contention in numerous advertising organizations. In the event that you accept that this variety is a work of art, at that point you will acknowledge and systematize variation — and it will be reflected in the expense of maintaining your business right now. If you accept that a lot of this variation is reasonable and the main drivers of variety can be diminished/dispensed with, you will decrease your working expenses and improve consumer satisfaction altogether. Yet, you need another perspective about these difficulties.

It is the methodology of Six Sigma that makes it one of a kind. The measurable instruments utilized in the Six Sigma process are not new. Be that as it may, these apparatuses have as of late gained increased practical application because of the development of computer software and hardware, so as to place the tools under the control of the majority. One of the key segments of Six Sigma is the methodology of Define, Measure, Analyze, Improve, and Control (or DMAIC).

SIX SIGMA COMPONENTS

There are three fundamental ideas that are normal to all businesses that Six Sigma addresses: processes, defects, and variation. You might not have utilized these terms previously, yet we should take a gander at every one.

Process

A principal concept of Six Sigma is process. Any set of repetitive steps is a process—in any service, or transactional environment to accomplish some outcome. There are forms for the entirety of your center business exercises and capacities. They are the means that the individuals in your organization experience to carry out their responsibilities and have your services and products delivered. You might not have considered them, yet they're there. Getting them and making them work at the most elevated level conceivable is the objective of Six Sigma.

Defects

Some portion of the Six Sigma approach have to do with estimating a process for terms of defects. Six Sigma helps in eliminating defects so you can reliably and productively create and make delivery of items or service that meet and surpass your clients' desires. It's not surprising for an independent company to have at least 10 percent of its net gain being squandered by process defects. As it were, those defects are dollars squandered!

Variety

The Six Sigma strategy diminishes variations in business forms. It appears evident, however you can't reliably deliver a top notch item or service (your output) if variations are imbedded in your process, right? Fundamentally, you have accomplished six sigma when your process convey just 3.4 defects per million chances (DPMO). For instance, this would imply that out of one million bags checked in at the air terminal gear counter, just 3.4 would be lost. As it were, your processes are working superbly. Obviously, this is hard to do, yet you can start to move toward it (or if nothing else show signs of improvement) by executing the strategies depicted right now. The truth of the matter is that most organizations work at three to four sigma quality levels, which means around 25 percent of their income lost to defects in their process. Those damages or defects shows waste, rework, greater expenses, and disappointed clients. At what level of value level does your business work? Wouldn't you like to improve? Obviously you would! That is the thing that this book is about.

Since you have a starter comprehension of the essential concepts of Six Sigma, you might be asking "Can Six Sigma truly work for an independent venture?" The appropriate response is, Six Sigma can be executed in any business, paying little heed to what you do or how little you are. Six Sigma is about critical thinking and problem solving, and these problems are all over the place. It doesn't make a difference what type or size of business this breakthrough system is applied to. You may be a distributer, a retailer, a manufacturer or an organization made for service. You may have three workers, or perhaps you have 300. Regardless, Six Sigma will work for you.

THE KEY PRINCIPLES OF SIX SIGMA

The idea of Six Sigma has a straightforward objective – conveying near impeccable products and enterprises for business change and for ideal consumer satisfaction

Focus on the Customer

This depends on the prevalent view that the "client is the ruler." The essential objective is to carry most extreme advantage to the client. For this, a business needs to understand its clients, their needs, and what drives deals or reliability. This requires setting up the standard of value as characterized by what the client or market requests.

Measure the Value Stream and Find Your Problem

A given business process steps should be mapped to know regions of waste. Assemble information to find the particular area of problem that will be tended to or changed. Have objectives or goals clearly defined for information gathering, including defining the information to be gathered, the explanation behind the information gathering, bits of knowledge expected, guaranteeing the precision of estimations, and setting up an institutionalized information collection framework. Find out if the information is assisting with accomplishing the objectives, regardless of whether the information should be refined, or extra data gathered. Recognize the issue. Pose inquiries and discover the underlying cause.

Dispose of the Junk

When the problem or issue is recognized, make changes to the process to remove variation, consequently expelling defects. Expel the activities in the process that don't add to the client value. In the event that the value stream doesn't uncover where the problem or issue lies, techniques or tools are utilized to help find the exceptions and issue territories. Streamline capacities to accomplish quality control and productivity. At last, by taking out the previously mentioned junk, bottlenecks in the process are eliminated.

Keep the Ball Rolling

Include all partners. Embrace an organized procedure where your group contributes and make collaborations using their various skills for problem solving or critical thinking. Six Sigma procedures can greatly affect a business or organization, so the group must be capable in the standards and systems utilized. Subsequently, knowledge and trainings which are highly specialized are required to lessen the danger of venture or re-plan disappointments and guarantee that the process performs ideally.

Guarantee a Flexible and Responsive Ecosystem

The quintessence of Six Sigma is business transformation and change. At the point when a defective or wasteful procedure is evacuated, it requires an adjustment in the work practice and approach of the employee. A vigorous culture of flexibility and responsiveness to changes in techniques can guarantee streamlined task execution. The individuals and offices included ought to have the option to adjust to change easily, so to encourage this, process ought to be intended for brisk and easy adoption. Eventually, the organization that has an eye fixed on the information analyzes the main concern intermittently and changes its process where essential, can increase its competitive edge.

HOW LEAN AND SIX SIGMA ARE INTERTWINED

Lean Six Sigma uses approaches from both Lean and Six Sigma to cut costs of production, improve quality, accelerate, remain competitive, and set aside cash. From Six Sigma, organizations profit by the decreased variations on parts. Likewise, Lean sets aside cash for the organization by concentrating on the sorts of waste and how to lessen such waste. The two procedures meet up into Lean Six Sigma, making a very much adjusted and sorted out solution for saving profits and produce better items.

Albeit Lean and Six Sigma are various processes, they are corresponding and share numerous similitudes that permit them to go together in a seamless manner In this way, they have been joined. The likenesses permit them to work together well. The distinctions guarantee that there are explanatory techniques and solution alternatives accessible, that will improve the process, item or service. It is because of the likenesses that the two kinds of analysis should be possible at the same time on a similar procedure, item, or administration.

Initially, both Lean and Six Sigma stress the way that the client determine the item or servicce. This implies when process are analyzed, the significance or need of steps in the process ought to be inspected through the eyes of the client. Likewise, Lean and Six Sigma use process flow maps in order to get an understanding of the production flow and distinguish any waste. Moreover, both depend on information to figure out which parts of production need improvement in productivity and to quantify the achievement of upgrades. At long last, because of actualizing Lean and Six Sigma, productivity normally improves and variation diminishes. Effectiveness and variation go together, with progress in one bringing about an improvement in the other. More on the similarities are;

- Both depend on information for deciding state of current execution and for determining the impact of future execution. The information gathered in a Lean Six Sigma task can regularly be utilized to help both Lean investigation and Six Sigma analysis. The dependence on information assists with guaranteeing that the real cause is found.

- Both are applied utilizing improvement projects that regularly will be executed by a little cross functional group. The project duration and team size will rely on the degree and size of the process, product or service being investigated for development.

- Both have moved past the manufacturing activity and are presently utilized for all business functions and for inter and external facing processes. They are additionally utilized in all enterprises including mechanical, consumer, government, training, and non-profits.

- Improvement which depends on utilizing either approach will both diminish waste and lessen variations. Expelling wasted steps and activates (muda) disposes variations sources, and eliminating these variations kills the capacity of wasted processes and steps related with keeping the variations (mura and muri).

However, there are a few contrasts in the two methodologies. These distinctions don't make a contention, rather they give numerous ways that can be utilized to arrive at a comparative goal. A Lean Six Sigma undertaking should let the defect nature, as determined by the value of the client, and the present condition of the process of the business, item, or service show which forms of techniques are most proper. The solution is regularly a blend of both Lean and Six Sigma improvements.

What is the distinction between Lean and Six Sigma?

- Diverse concentration for identification of problems – Lean is centered around waste (muda, mura, muri) and

Six Sigma is centered around variations, any deviation from the objective performance.

- Various sorts of techniques– Lean principally utilizes visual strategies for both analysis and for creating solutions that are bolstered with information analysis. Six Sigma fundamentally utilizes measurable tools or techniques for analysis and creation solutions that are bolstered with information visualization. A myth is then generated that Lean is simpler than Six Sigma, on the grounds that the visual analysis of Lean is straightforward, while numerous individuals are scared by Six Sigma's numerical examination. Actually the two kinds of examination are anything but difficult to perform with the present statistical support instruments.

- Various sorts of documentation for the solution – the solution provided by Lean is reported with a reexamined value stream map that prompts changes in work processes and frequently changes in work directions at many of the process steps. The Six Sigma arrangement is archived with changes in set up techniques and the control plan for observing the process and reacting to variations. It will likewise affect work directions and as often as possible prompts changes in the measurements approach or frameworks.

The two methodologies are good from multiple points of view that it was anything but difficult to consolidate them into one methodology in order to get the synergistic impact of joining them. Lean Six Sigma, as it is regularly practised, maintains a strategic distance from pitfalls of approaches which failed before.

LEAN SIX SIGMA PRINCIPLES

Outline of the principle that have assisted with making Lean Six Sigma so compelling.

Addressing a real world problem

Lean Six Sigma is both a top-down and base-up methodology. The top-down component is related with problem determination. The Lean Six Sigma projects groups are centered around real world issues that are affecting clients and process at same time. Frequently, the colleagues are feeling the impact of the issue with rework and repair activities or tending to client grievances. This create a sense of necessity and importance to the project. It isn't simply "busy work," it is genuine work. It is regularly difficult to get the business to perceive the significance of this strategy for business success. Purchase-in is a lot simpler to accomplish when both business management and the group comprehend the significance of distinguishing and fixing the problem. In any case, the executives don't dictate a problem and the necessary solution. It is the analysis by the group decides the genuine cause.

Analysis is accomplished by a group

A Lean Six Sigma project is typically staffed by a cross-useful group that is engaged with various parts of the process being dissected. Numerous business forms are cross-functional and an analysis which is cross-functional is expected to forestall sub-optimization of the process. Improving one stage to the detriment of another progression doesn't dispose of waste or variation, it just moves it to an alternate step in the process. Including a cross-functional group will make all the points of view of the organization that are involved and affected by the undertaking to be included in analysis of the problem, and much more significantly in the improvement of the solution.

The different team member possessing in-depth knowledge is useful for understanding the issue and the data implications. These alternate points of view are critical to enable the group to provide a solution that solve the immediate problem and regularly, will assist with wiping out waste and variations in different parts of the process.

Analysis is centered around a process

Lean Six Sigma is best utilized for breaking down process. In any event, when the issue under scrutiny is an undeniable product problem, Lean Six Sigma will be considerably more powerful when it is applied to the process that plans or builds the product, as opposed to taking a look at the item itself. That is on the grounds that the analysis is intended to research and improve activities, and activities are the means of processes. In a vacuum, activities rarely happen with no effect from preceding or succeeding activities. Rather they should be considered with regards to the process in which they are happening. The Lean value stream map or Six Sigma process map give an image of that process.

Analysis depends on data

Lean Six Sigma depends on data, not guesses. The Lean value stream map is confirmed with a stroll through of the process, and afterward information is gathered at each progression. The present state of the process, product or service is estimated in the Measure stage. This incorporates having the problem or defect measured and estimating whatever is done effectively. The information that is gotten is utilized for analysis to find out the real condition of what's going on, not an assumed state. The analysis done checks the basic causes with the goal that the right issue is fixed. In any case, the dependence on data doesn't stop there. At the point when a solution has been made, data is gathered to decide whether the solution has genuinely fixed the issue. And afterward, data is utilized to guarantee the solution remains set up and the problem doesn't return.

Understand the effect of the process sigma

This next rule is centered around the analysis of the Six Sigma. The viable effect of sigma is that it shows the measure of ordinary variation that happens. It is constantly attached to a particular parameter or trademark that is being measured. Same properties of an item or process will have no variation. That trait never shows signs of change, regardless of how frequently the item or process happens. Different attributes do have variations. There is a normal value, however there is no certainty about a particular example. Sigma is the factual estimation of that uncertainty.

- The limits for a little more than 66% of the events is represented by one sigma

- Two sigma represents 95% of the events.

- Three sigma represents over 99% of the events.

- When you get out to six sigma, there are just around 3 possibilities in a million that ordinary variations could cause the attribute being estimated to be different from the normal value.

Sigma shows variation, it says nothing regarding acceptability. Notice that the reference to the quality being estimated is satisfactory from a client or viewpoint which is standard. A quality could have a little sigma, basically no variation. If the normal estimated value of that quality is outside the limits of what the client finds satisfactory, it just implies that it is constantly damaged. By a similar token, a characteristic or attribute could have an exceptionally huge sigma, there is an elevated level of uncertainty. If the client has no particular expectations concerning the attribute, it will consistently be accepted, paying little heed to the variation.

Solution addresses to the real root cause(s)

Lean Six Sigma is one of the most dominant critical thinking, problem solving and persistent improvement procedures since it distinguishes and points out the attributes of the real problem. A few methodologies start with the assumption that each issue has an extraordinary or uncommon cause, and if that cause can be recognized and disposed of or controlled, the problem leaves. Different techniques start with the supposition that the issue is a typical occurrence inside the process. The process is defective fundamentally or lacking and if the process were changed to evade this defect or address this deficiency, the problem leaves.

The two objectives are admirable and in certainty are quite comparable. The best approach to fix the primary issue is to place a "spot correction" to control the cause which is unique, and the fix for the subsequent methodology is to re-engineer the process. Choosing an inappropriate solution technique, unfortunately, doesn't improve the circumstance and can exacerbate the situation. Lean Six Sigma utilizes the instruments to determine whether the issue is a unique cause or a typical cause. By making this differentiation, the group can proceed to locate the genuine underlying cause or causes. Likewise, the group can make a solution system that will properly address the problem. It can be a special cause. In this case, a special solution can be implemented. In the event that it is a typical reason, the process can be redesigned.

Solution includes a control system to enable it "stick"

Lean Six Sigma doesn't end with recognizing the problem or even with providing a solution. The last phase of Lean Six Sigma is the Control stage. Natural resistance to change can be seen in most organizations. For some individuals and systems, change is hard. Propensities must be broken, new strategies acquired, new data is required. In the Lean Six Sigma Control stage, there is implementation of the solution and the business starts to utilize it. While this is going on, the project group is guaranteeing the entirety of the supporting frameworks are likewise given an update to mirror any changes and they give coaching and trainings to process managers and supervisors on the utilization of the solution. This include making sure the control systems that have the process being monitored, are set up to identify if the process starts to return to the past behaviour. Victory is not declared by the project group and disband on the grounds that they have effectively shown their solution once. They tend to stay with it through a significant number of occurrences, statistically. This both exhibits the solution truly tackled the issue and that the managers and operators are prepared and ready to deal with the improved process.

ADVANTAGES OF LEAN SIX SIGMA FOR YOUR BUSINESS

Lean Six Sigma gives different advantages to businesses. It sets aside cash, yet in addition, changes the frame of mind of employees and the usefulness of the organization. Lean Six Sigma is a persistent improvement approach. In any case, a genuine inquiry is, what does it improve? Does it make sales or profit to increase? Does it improve consumer satisfaction and reduce complaints? Does it lower costs, improve incoming quality, outgoing quality or the expense of quality? Does it improve worker confidence? Does it increase your compensation and benefits, or improve your promotability? "Yes" to these.

Through usage of Lean Six Sigma, businesses can anticipate the following gainful results:

ORGANIZATIONAL BENEFITS

Lean Six Sigma is a nonstop improvement approach for a business. So, there is an anticipation of organization benefits. We should think about the idea of the advantages and their suggestion.

Simple Processes

Lean Six Sigma will improve the business forms. The cross-functional value stream maps will distinguish territories of waste and ineffectiveness. A considerable lot of the processes have implanted rework and work-arounds for problems which are persistent. At the point when the wasted effort is expelled and the rework and workarounds are never again required, the rest of the processes are straightforward and a lot simpler to oversee and control. A faster process is achieved by this, which prompts better client assistance, service and higher consumer satisfaction. Both of those will ordinarily prompt more prominent deals. Also, the more straightforward, quicker process will bring down overhead costs which will build benefits. At long last, more straightforward processes have less opportunities for mistakes. Accordingly, they typically are seen as of higher quality and less defects.

Less errors and mistakes

Look further into that advantage of less errors and mix-ups. Lean Six Sigma begins with a meaning of a quality that is acceptable, dependent on what the client's value. The spotlight on quality, externally, prioritize continuous improvement effort to address the issues that have the most effect on business achievement. Likewise, the dependence on information to have problems defined rather than gut feeling further organizes the improvement exertion on the genuine issues in the association. The outcome is that the upgrades fix genuine problems and carry them to a level that is worthy to the genuine clients. Thus, it isn't only that Lean Six Sigma tends to blunders and missteps in the business, but instead that Lean Six Sigma tends to address errors matter.

Predictable Performance

Basic processes are simpler to control and oversee than complex processes, particularly those processes with less mistakes and errors. However, added to these advantages, Lean Six Sigma has an attention on lessening variations inside a process. With less variations, processes become progressively predictable. That implies cycle duration, quality output and expenses, which are all predictable. What's more, these can prompt better customer care, less complaints, and good profits. This consistency turns into a great advantage for an organization while working in a situation of moving changes at fast pace. Changing innovation and client desires are now making a precarious business condition. Without processes which can't be predicted, it is practically difficult to make and actualize a suitable response to this instability.

Active control

The Lean Six Sigma technique makes the cycle time short and sets up constant information-based control plans and frameworks. With short cycle times and information-based control frameworks, the managers as well as operators can settle on choices that make great impact on performance. The performance, worker spirit, and agility are all improved. The managers see how their work impacts the process performance and they get quick feedback. The operators are more averse to feel that they are casualties of the process since they are currently engaged with dealing with the process and improving it. With short cycles and dynamic control, the business can rapidly react to circumstances in the evolving marketplace. Furthermore, short productive processes that are recorded with the value stream maps and control graphs are simpler to get them updated than complex undocumented processes.

PERSONAL BENEFITS

Lean Six Sigma gives advantages to people in the organization who become Lean Six Sigma pioneers. Some of the individual advantages you can expect while taking part in Lean Six Sigma.

Personal Effectiveness

Lean Six Sigma gives an organized problem solving and critical thinking methodology that can be utilized to address any sort of issue. Having the option to discover and fix issues will improve your capacity to act in any position and industry. The Lean Six Sigma system steers you through a composed process of request, analysis, problem identification and creation of solution. A considerable lot of the instruments and techniques can be applied to ordinary problems. Yet, regardless of whether you don't utilize all the tools, the well-organized problem-solving approach will place you in charge of finding and fixing your issues.

Leadership Opportunity

Lean Six Sigma is executed through tasks and such tasks have those in lead. Being the leader of a Lean Six Sigma project will frequently give a chance for introduction to different functions and senior administration. This form of introduction is with regards to somebody who can discover and fix an issue. Associating with colleagues and managers will probably improve your communication and basic leadership aptitudes. The structure of Lean Six Sigma can assist you with developing your project skills involving management. What's more, obviously having the option to put on your resume that you were the leader of a project group that accomplished cost reserve funds, quality improvement, and cycle duration decrease will just help you as you look for that next advancement or new opportunity.

Pay and promotability

Which carries us to the compensation and promotability of Lean Six Sigma professionals. Achieving belt affirmation is an important qualification on your resume. Many occupation postings, necessitate that a candidate have a Lean Six Sigma qualification. Along these lines, this will open the entryway for certain advancements. What's more, inside an organization, advancements are regularly founded on how you have exhibited your leadership abilities. Viably driving a Lean Six Sigma venture shows senior administration and HR that you are prepared for more prominent duty. The normal for your industry and nation will fluctuate. However, it is safe to say that your earning potential will be enhanced by Lean Six Sigma certification.

TACTICS TO GROW YOUR BUSINESS THE LEAN SIGMA WAY

Make the Most Out of Time

Time is a troublesome easily overlooked detail that likes to hinder enormous advancement. Assembling improvement for a process is troublesome, particularly when things have just begun and everybody is profound into their employments and plans. So, gather as a lot of information as you can and sort it. This

will assist you with concentrating on what the most concerning issues are. Discover the numbers and figure out what they mean. What is your input and output? Who are your suppliers and merchants?

Find a workable relationship with your employee(s) and supervisory crews and discover how they work best. Do they do well in gatherings or produce more without anyone else's input? Attempt to oblige your employees in the manner that makes them increasingly compelling and beneficial.

Invest in Software

Since you have your arrangements together and everybody ready, it's a great opportunity to put resources into some quality programming software suites. Utilize a homegrown framework programming that gives valuable data and graphically shows statistics for your projects. To expand the viability of these product suites, group Verizon FIOS web network with other essential services to set aside cash and streamline things for your bookkeeping sect. Gain all that you can from one program before you proceed onward to the following, yet don't make due with one that possibly offers one support in the event that you need six more. When you have innovation on your side, it's a great opportunity to get down to business.

Spread Your Resources Evenly

Focus on your new plans. Utilize the measure of labor and assets you have to do the entirety of your projects and thoughts. The key is to not be inefficient with them. In the event that you just need five individuals to work on something, don't utilize six. This will keep payrolls reasonable and project running easily in light of the fact that you don't have one individual getting in every other person's way. Find or train somebody with a vital view for your business who can come in and show staff before your first project. Concentrate on your clients. Without them, there's no demand. The purpose of an improved strategy is to keep clients fulfilled and returning for additional, which develops your business.

Take note of a go-to person inside the organization who has a vital perspective on your business. A process expert can come in and help instruct the team before your first project, or you can have somebody inside your organization get formal preparing. You'll likewise need to help any employee fundamentally associated with a quality-improvement program with temporary laborers who can take on a portion of their normal task at hand.

Understand your Organization Culture

Are your kin individualistic or collaborative? An organization of people may not give it a second thought, nor see, how to work with others; you'll need additional time and motivating forces to pick up their interest in process improvement.

Trust in Your System and Analyze It

When you have everything begun, you need to keep up along these lines of working or everything will be put to waste. You can create training classes, regularly to show new employees how to function in your business. Use as much as you can from your resources before joining more. Have the labor to keep things beneficial — not untidy. Keep your eyes on the numbers and other significant data so you can keep them from declining before it's past the point of no return.

Most importantly, focus on the client.

The purpose of any process improvement methodology is to improve your output to fulfill clients, and subsequently develop your business. Effect on the client ought to be a basic piece of any procedure documentation.

Win the Race

Organizations who actually believe in and make use of the Lean Six Sigma methodology are organizations that are endeavoring toward the decrease of waste and inefficiencies. With six sigma, an organization will have just 3.4 defects per million. What client would be insane to give their cash to some other business? With more effectiveness and better resources, any business can embrace the six sigma way of thinking and draw in those customers.

Difficult work and devotion will make this program work for any business, yet it's not constantly a stroll in the recreation center. There will most likely be obstructions and deterrents for you to sway and weave through. When you turn out the entirety of your problems, it ought to be a smooth ride to the highest point of the business. So, don't get debilitated and be keen by preparing, utilizing appropriate trainings and practical strategies to enable you to succeed. Six Sigma or some other process improvement approach is in itself a long-term effort. Try not to expect results tomorrow, or even one month from now – but maintaining commitment regularly and quality improvement will pay off after some time.

CHAPTER THREE: BUSINESS APPLICATION OF LEAN SIX SIGMA

Taking a look at many organizations in the United states, about 84% of all, have less than 50 employees. The figure is at a comparative level over the world. SMEs represent 60 to 70% of employments in many nations, and they additionally represent an excessively huge portion of new openings. The failure rate is additionally high for small businesses, unfortunately.

A small organization may not understand the gigantic returns of that of an organization which is large, however that doesn't lessen the effect of a quality program's return on investment. The issue is that everyday tasks frequently redirect the business proprietor's consideration from what is useful for the organization in the long haul, permitting just a little time (assuming any) to plan and forestalling problems.

Studies have indicated that there are a few highlights that are regular to all high growth SMEs:

- Innovation: those who are innovators grow quicker than non-pioneers

- Attention to HR: At the prior stages, the managerial abilities and motivation for employees are critical for survival.

- Emphasis on techniques which relates to enhancing, updating, or growing the current product line, and improving production. Fast growing business enthusiasts which are successful are those that make an interpretation of their vital emphases without hesitation.

- Emphasis on enlisting employees that are skilled and training them

- Balance, an emphasis on working to improve their abilities in every area.

Each organization must make sure clients, partners, and workers are satisfied in order to grow and survive, yet some small organizations have little support to shield clients from mistakes and waste, which is the reason implementing quality projects that keep this from happening, is a choice that can help entrepreneurs towards accomplishing these 5 destinations simultaneously: Six Sigma rely upon the skills of individuals to grow new tasks. These tasks will bring development and improve production, which will spur employees and upgrade capacities in all areas.

The best time to start and deploy a quality program is during the startup stage involving planning so as to consolidate quality into the item and service. This can however be actualized whenever, as long as everyone is ready, particularly the executives.

Six Sigma is one of the few quality systems that can be applied from the earliest starting point, and could bring about high reserve funds, particularly in business that produce a high volume of standard items or services consistently. The initial step to begin executing Six-Sigma is to have the management team and all the workers, trained on the basics of Six Sigma and the DMAIC strategy, which will enable the organization to begin improving all its project and actualizing theory immediately. There are other basic success factors required for effective execution of Lean Six Sigma in your business. These elements are required for utilizing lean or Six Sigma as solitary projects, as well. The need for official level engagement is the first of these factors.

Management at the senior level must be in control, reliably strong, and ready to assume a functioning role in communication and reward. Lean Six Sigma must be viewed as a social move, not the most recent program-of the-month. Senior management must guarantee linkage of Lean Six Sigma to corporate techniques by using powerful goal deployment and performance-tracking strategies. They should give clear prioritization comparative with different activities, projects, and priorities. Senior management must learn various strategies for settling on choices from those they have utilized previously. Basically, all degrees of basic leadership must utilize realities and information to help actions. They should comprehend and depend on statistics for deciphering and having data clarified. What's more, one of the results of focusing on fact and information based decisions is that management and the business should build up a resilience for challenging company beliefs that are sacred. The customary hierarchical view should be supplanted with an outside spotlight on clients and their viewpoints. Senior management must build up responsibility and make standing definitions on expectations, jobs, and duties regarding the organization. Senior management will be liable for directing and taking an interest in normally planned reviews to guarantee and confirm progress of the Lean Six Sigma projects.

Communication is another basic success factor. There must be standard composed communications on Lean Six Sigma news and successes. Aids for communication are developed and disseminated for the executives. A typical language is made and advocated dependent on Lean Six Sigma. Lean Six Sigma is promoted visibly in each organization meeting and communication. Another component of successful projects that is not entirely obvious is the requirement for making and communicating a Human Resource plan to help the different roles for Lean Six Sigma.

The following basic success factor is simply the project. A project pipeline over one year must be made and constantly revived. The project must be connected to basic business and client needs. The project's extension and size must be identified so as to deliver critical investment funds and still be attainable. Other resources which are important should be doled out. It has likewise been discovered useful to execute a project-tracking system that will help keep projects on track by making their (or deficiency in that department) noticeable.

The following framework can likewise be utilized to convey projects results so the information picked up from one can be applied in different areas.

Other basic success factor for Lean Six Sigma is the requirement for core knowledge and abilities in an assortment of areas, including:

- Having Information on system and value streams. How related parts progress in the direction of a common aim. The objective is to upgrade value-added segments while having variations reduced with the goal that clients consistently get what they need.

- Information on different instruments. Analysis of data, statistics, quality strategies, root cause analysis, lean techniques, etc. Groups should have the option to recognize signal from commotion, identify genuine root cause, propose countermeasures, create improvement plans, and propel the project to the finish following organized techniques.

- Information on brain research. The skills which include; interpersonal and managerial, are needed to sell ideas, motivate groups, settle on information-based choices, manage conflict, and create trust.

KICKSTARTING YOUR BUSINESS THE LEAN SIX SIGMA WAY

The topic of where to begin isn't as perplexing as it would appear. The appropriate response lies in the sorts of projects your business or organization will discover most advantageous, what you are attempting to accomplish with your providers and clients, and the preparedness of your organization to follow up on these chances. Recall that the motivation behind your first improvement project is to make the conditions for social change just as quantifiable and important improvement to consumer satisfaction, cost, speed, or different elements. Your decision of initial projects will figure out which toolbox to utilize, however whichever you pick, it is essential to simply begin.

However, it is simplest to choose where to begin if you recollect that lean projects and Six Sigma tasks can be utilized as reciprocal advances. For instance, if the quickest need is to improve the cycle duration of an activity, eliminate errors from certain steps, or better organize work process, the regular place to begin would be with a lean task. If the procedure is now sorted out and in charge and now the client is increasingly keen on decreasing the variations in on-time shipments or item defects, Six Sigma would be good. From that point onward, you may find that a specific procedure step requires an excessive amount of work-in-process stock to look after uptime: back to lean.

THINGS TO CONSIDER

Consider a Wide Variety of Improvement Needs, Then Choose Carefully

Your improvement needs ought to be unequivocally attached to the key strategies of the business and be measurable. Potential projects list ought to be created and considered by the management group. While it is enticing to attempt a wide assortment of projects; some lean, some Six Sigma, some both, across departments, this is generally not the best first course. Rather, select a particular area of business that has a couple of basic goals and estimations that can be improved by utilizing project groups that will promptly give support to one another and give a synergistic outcome. Presently, do these projects look like lean, Six Sigma, or both? Spare the remainder of that rundown of incredible project ideas for the following round. In the first round of projects it is generally critical to exhibit some extraordinary triumphs and afterward develop your usage into different areas.

Consider Your Customers and Suppliers

Is it true that you are on a similar group with your clients and suppliers? Assuming this is the case, what might cause your business to perform better within the entire supply chain? You will increase a ton of good reputation by asking your clients and in any event, including them in your projects, directly. In like manner, by teaching your providers through some underlying projects, you have the chance to improve the production network coming into your organization. Indeed, getting both your suppliers and clients engaged with your efforts and activities will be important in completing your Lean Six Sigma venture.

In any case, don't fall into the snare of requesting more from your suppliers than your own business is willing and ready to do. Your suppliers will judge how serious your intent is by the activities of your organization. Setting the example by the quality, pace, and consequences of your tasks will build up motivation instead of hatred. In reality, when both your organization and your supplier succeed together, the advantages will be most noteworthy. All things considered, when searching for process upgrades, the best ones may frequently be found in the organizational interfaces.

Develop Six Sigma Strategy and Deployment Plan

Numerous organizations live by the improvement myth that the business or organization must learn as it goes. What is the consequence of this myth? At the point when you walk through a guileless organization that practices this methodology, each supervisor has a white board with their own rundown of Six Sigma ventures brainstormed which support the program. Every ha a customized checklist code to go about monitoring progress and a little border drawn around it. In some cases, there is such a great amount of stuff on their sheets you wonder how they even get to know about it. notification it. Once every week they all gather together to go through their list. If you have an interview with all the managerial crew and duplicate their rundowns, you discover techniques which are disconnected, conflicts, redundancies, contradiction, blame dealing, and "simply making a cursory effort." There is this enormous misinterpretation that the volume of movement or various forms of activity and the speed of perceived completion are relative to the final results.

Six Sigma isn't a business system. It is one of numerous empowering influences to accomplish the business technique. Despite everything, organizations must thoroughly consider the subtleties of how they will improve the business by means of Six Sigma. Albeit a large number of the Six Sigma statistical tools depend on possibility or chance, an effective Six Sigma deployment involves decision. Numerous businesses avoid the most significant component of improvement: the Six Sigma procedure and plan of deployment. Organizations general skim over this procedure and jump into the tools and methodologies. Individuals select and execute techniques and tools with an end goal to get speedy outcomes. Their goals are acceptable in light of the fact that they are attempting to have a brisk effect, yet their activities and proposed actions are bad on the grounds that they wind up pursuing results since they don't have a strong improvement plan. The anxiety associated with jumping in, leaves the remainder of the organization's in perplexity and uncertainty, initially. Without a Six Sigma technique and plan of deployment that is well-defined, activities are "perception driven" versus "fact driven" and not concentrated on strategic gaps and actual causes of poor performance. The vast majority of the attention is on scheduling wave after influx of Six Sigma training and the compulsory projects are an untimely idea. This methodology may deliver a couple of momentary advantages, yet it never turns into a process which is sustaining. A more intensive look normally uncovers disengagement between client necessities and the organization's daily improvement activities. The outcomes are inevitably sketchy and illusive, and before you know it, they are casualties of another "flavor of-the-month" improvement program. For the employees of these organizations, acquainting them with Six Sigma gets about as a lot of excitement as passing a mononucleosis culture around.

Once more, we have to inquire as to why. The appropriate response is a similar explanation as above. Key improvement is a vital competency that administrators need to develop and create on the grounds that it is a new concept to them. Having dealing with change is vague, even at best. All things considered, a proper Six Sigma system is absent in three-quarters of the organizations seeking after Six Sigma.

Building up a strong Six Sigma technique and improvement plan is complicated. There is a lot of research involved, and also, thought and time to put a decent functional improvement plan together. More often than not, there are huge pressure to get things going now, so the plan is distorted because individuals think they comprehend what should be done. Speed can be an amazingly destructive form of decision especially if organizations decide to take a shortcut on the most basic strides of improvement. Great leaders perceive that it required some investment of time and current thinking to get into the circumstance, and it will require some ample time, diverse reasoning, and steadiness to change the circumstance.

Organizations will never understand the outcomes they expect without this well-defined Six Sigma procedure and deployment plan. This turns into the vision, objectives, and implementation instrument by which they can convey why, and what requirements to change. A decent improvement plan likewise responds to numerous inquiries and concerns various individuals may have about change and how certain issues will be taken care of. Without a doubt, it doesn't have all the appropriate responses contained inside it, yet it turns into an extraordinary objective to take shots at, grasp, deploy, and execute. In addition, it gives structure and sense of formality to the initiative of Six Sigma and an incredible litmus test for Six Sigma activities.

Consider the Organization's Readiness

Are there experiences gained by you in your organization involving the tools and techniques of either lean or Six Sigma? Provided that this is true, you should exploit this in your first choice of resources and projects. Does your organization now see the need for speed in the process flow? This can be an extraordinary propelling point for lean. Or does your organization have workers with technical knowhow in statistics and control of processes and can handle the power of Six Sigma statistics? This could get Six Sigma off to a noteworthy beginning.

Mandate Linkage to the Business Plan

Best Six Sigma endeavors are driven by an official steering group that create linkage between key needs and Six Sigma activity. This steering group usually provide a direction of Six Sigma which is usually broad, to the organization on very important areas which require improvement. Most additionally have a conventional procedure of getting potential activities through a litmus test in order to place strategic importance on priority. Some even manage the measure of action in progress at some random time, so Six Sigma doesn't take on its very own existence like past improvement programs.

This methodology forestalls the projects for the project's sake syndrome and limits nonvalue-added Six Sigma action. Numerous organizations are guilty, yet may not be happy to admit it. For instance, there have been a few cases in organizations where their unique Six Sigma objectives are supplanted by the mechanics of the procedure itself. They see organization as choosing candidates, appointing projects, scheduling trainings and giving reports on statistics which are meaningless. Regularly, applicants are allotted Six Sigma projects that are not really that of Six Sigma projects by any means. Activity doesn't generally convert into progress. A conventional linkage to the business strategy is helpful, yet it should be adjusted by the effort required to accomplish this linkage. It certainly causes individuals to get their work done before setting out on a project since they know the steering committee board of trustees has its finger on the beat of Six Sigma.

Establish Recognition of the Need

One of the greatest challenges associated with leadership is to keep officials and the whole organizations focused. Numerous business executives have a full plate of needs, and regularly key improvement is lower on their rundown than other needs which are more pressing. A few organizations defer change and expectation the economy will deal with things. Change is a reactive event as opposed to a proactive living event. At times executives start a vital initiative like Six Sigma and go ahead to break the momentum needed for change, unintentionally. This is done by hitting the remote-control improvement button, having to celebrate success at the initial stage, excessively long, or just proceeding onward to different needs (which sends a solid message that something different is progressively significant). It is extremely hard to glance at reality in the face, and the main response is a string of denial musings and feelings or to accuse suppliers, clients, or another person. Another basic event is the debate which continues talking about what is needed to be done. This creates a sense of confusion and conflicts in direction relating to change.

The truth of the matter is, regardless of where your present performance lies, it is essentially not good enough. Simply consider the hundreds or thousands of associations that have been market leaders just to give up that position to one who is a competitor within twelve to two years. The economy worldwide, is moving at clock speed, innovation and product life cycles are short, and everybody is associated with business improvement. Clients are constantly sourcing quicker, better, less expensive suppliers around the world. The bar is being raised at a lot quicker speed than numerous organizations can keep up with. However, this additionally gives the chance to leap frog and shock the competition with the correct strategy. The best time to change is now, but this mostly require an event which is usually catastrophic to prime the organizational pump for change. This is rather unfortunate. It is significantly simpler to create a sense of urgency with the use of a catastrophic occurrence rather than leadership; however, it frequently makes you late for the gathering. What is intermittent is Calamity driven improvement. The proportion of organizations that change because of proactive leadership is a lot of lower than associations that change because of a calamitous occasion. Without a strong acknowledgment of the

need to change, improvement programs are regularly reactionary and brief, and the outcomes are likewise baffling.

Another piece of this is getting the organization to "think big and remain hungry." Stretch goals and quicker celebrations are included. This incorporates stretch objectives and celebrations in quick succession followed by working up mindfulness that the organization can improve. The goal is to discover balance between saluting groups on their triumphs and tossing down new difficulties for them to meet. It is better nowadays to proactively increase current standards than to have your opposition force it in your organization.

Incorporate Enterprise-Wide Scope

Each business or organization has opportunities of improvement all through the whole organisation. Taking a closer look at the causal variables of client issues or unsatisfactory performance confirms this reality. Frequently, the root causes involving performance in assembling, sales, engineering, finance, or client service lie outside of these regions. We are not encouraging apportioning blames. This is because a large number of these root cause are well within the control of these areas. Nonetheless, business forms are cross-functional, where throughout the organization, the performance of the whole is subject to processes touchpoints.

Intending to Succeed

Effective Lean Six Sigma begins with a well-structured form but a plan which is flexible and realistic. The need to increase early understanding and responsibility is high, and projects must be effectively followed up with discipline. At last, everybody should be completely dedicated to a total and thorough course of action. A common Lean Six Sigma execution may advance through six unmistakable stages:

- Vision and communication. An unmistakable and convincing vision must be recognized, imparted, and acknowledged by partners. What is the ideal result for the activities, for the business, and for the client? What money related advantages must be accomplished to legitimize the pledge to Lean Six Sigma? What quantifiable advantages will clients find in cost, speed, and quality?

- Focus, structure and education. Since compelling and effective teamwork is basic for effective projects, having roles and responsibilities with training, is as significant as specialized skill improvement. Durable, cross-functional groups should be supported. Champions which are supportive are basic to this procedure and ought to have the option to evacuate obstructions; groups must consider their project to be as a critical business need. All colleagues should commit time and effort to make their project effective and will profit by consistent support of their endeavors and special roles.

- Define key metrics. An arrangement of metrics, or key indicators for perforrmance, will show progress in satisfying the vision of the implementation and accomplishing explicit objectives.

  This framework ought to be built up early in implementation since projects ought to be chosen to improve these pointers in a collective manner.

- Basic Lean Six Sigma tool deployment. Early projects may require just the fundamentals of lean and Six

Sigma and give the speedy and unmistakable outcomes that an organization needs in order for it to gain experience and build an enthusiastic spirit. Making use of visual controls and institutionalized work is a decent beginning stage. 5S (sort, set in order, shine, standardized, sustain) will get the show on the road toward an exceptionally profitable work space. With Six Sigma, process mapping, defects classification and causes, and essential speculation testing and analysis of data might be all that are required for projects initially.

- Advance tool deployment. As groups gain experience, further developed techniques, for example, productive maintenance, mistake proofing, kanban, experiments design and advanced statistics may be good. The compensations for utilizing these tools which are advanced may include ground breaking achievements and discoveries that will invigorate the project groups further and identify ideas for new projects.

- Move to whole value stream. After progress is accomplished in a specialty unit or division with the essential instruments of Lean Six Sigma, the process of implementation should be moved to different regions. At this point, advanced tools can also be employed may likewise be utilized now where introductory projects require them. Best practices and philosophies ought to be reported and documented to make the execution as customized and significant as could reasonably be expected.

Great Project Management Is a Must!

The requirement for an implementation process which is successful can't be overemphasize. If there is need for the leaders of your initiative to make use of project management training, you have to perceive this as a basic arrangement of skills and have this training aspect built into the plan. At first, you will most likely have an eager group to work with. Be, as various projects unfurl, there will be an expanding number of duties to make. Certain people may feel worn out on the thoroughness required or the apparent clash with everyday work. For some organizations, the most ideal approach to neutralize these issues is to utilize formal task arranging strategies, including PERT and Gantt diagrams. If you utilize these tools with discipline, the continuous responsibility and duty you need will be overseen precisely, appropriately, and well. All things considered, when the usage plan begins to slip, as definitely it will, you will need to utilize the 'individuals' side of your task management abilities. The basic skills will move from an accentuation on technical ability, and this success will rely intensely upon sincerity and profundity of top administration's dedication. Sustain this dedication altogether and in a continuous manner.

Getting Management Commitment

At some point or another in your usage, the degree of the executive's responsibility you accomplish will significantly influence the result. Know about the likelihood that some wary or incredulous leaders who from the outset don't seem to help your efforts may later end up being your greatest partners once they see good and tangible outcomes, while other people who show support feigning, before all else, may end up sabotaging the effort when they understand the degree of responsibility required.

Leadership and Mentoring are things that individuals state they realize how to do, yet they tumble down in real practice. For what reason does this occur? They need to be powerful leaders. However, vital improvement is a core competency that administrators need to develop and create in light of the fact that it is unfamiliar to them. Leaders who are good have the vision, conviction, certainty, and a stunning passionate determination to win regardless of what disrupts the general flow. They live, inhale, and comprehend the details of lean, kaizen, Six Sigma. They have an enthusiasm to succeed, and their fire-in-the-stomach duty is genuine. They put forth the attempt to instruct themselves like every other person.

They walk the talk and many handle a project like every other person. They have an astounding concern and enthusiasm for change and individuals. They put everything at risk and clarify that investment and achievement are the main choices. They superglue their official group together in solidarity of direction with a predictable message of progress. They adjust and recalibrate their associations and make a strong center of gravity. Perceive the contrast between realizing how to accomplish something and really doing it. Perceive the association's impediments and imperatives, and look for outside assistance to manage these issues as it so happens. You will make more prominent progress.

Three of the most ideal approaches to guarantee the management support are to:

- Training should be given at the early stage concentrated on setting up expectations for clear business results and estimations

- Adjust undertakings to help the requirements of each key supervisor's area of expertise, for instance, give an individual intrigue

- Demand frank and open conversation about implementation progress

At the point when it's a great opportunity to celebrate a good outcome, ensure that both the leaders who give the assets and the individuals from the Lean Six Sigma project groups are totally recognized and compensated.

Leveraging "The Language of Business"

Ensure that your plan is framed in the language of business — dollars and pennies, process durations, stock turns, return on investment, etc. Indeed, even consumer loyalty can be converted into these terms. At the point when a Lean Six Sigma venture is expending resources that can be estimated in these terms, it is crucial to show the potential or actual benefits a similar way.

Plan for an impressive future

Ensure that the organization builds up testing or 'leap forward' objectives. The methods for arriving at those objectives will rely upon arrangements that won't be evident from the outset or you would have

initiated them as of now. For instance, a goal to "lessen stock from $2.0 million to $1.9 million" won't get as a lot of help as "diminish stock by 50 percent" or even 90 percent. This is the place the estimation of Lean Six Sigma comes in, and clearly it will take some new reasoning! Stay away from any ventures that don't straightforwardly affect a top-level business objective. Simultaneously, you need to remember that so as to gain observable ground on a top-level objective, more than one or two projects might be required. Your best guide is to make each extend sufficiently little to be reachable in a sensible time with planned assets while synergizing with like tasks to have a quantifiable effect on those top objectives.

Communications

This should happen as often as possible and reliably at a few details: top-level program status, leadership review, and the status of individual group projects. A successful Lean Six Sigma usage ought to have an arrangement showing what sorts of communication are to be used (meetings, video, etc), who the crowds will be, who has the obligation regarding the communication, and due dates. A basic matrix will do the trick, distinguishing the kinds of planned communication in a left-hand section, trailed by the components of each in columns. Regardless of how the arrangement is spread out, the significant point will be to actualize it reliably. Top-level program communications can take different structures: worker meeting, organization pamphlets, organization occasions to commend achievement, and even pieces of the training program, for example, all-representative preparing on the essentials of Lean Six Sigma. Leadership review of all tasks ought to happen in any event month to month, while survey of the status of the general program ought to occur at any rate quarterly. Obviously, these time periods are rules and ought to be adjusted when needed. The fact of the matter is that these surveys will guarantee that the program remains on track and reacts to changes in business system that may happen now and again, and that the project groups keep on being considered responsible.

Soon after first experience with Lean Six Sigma, most business employees will be thinking about how projects are continuing. The information to be communicated which is very important include; updates for each task on the improvement to date, the present phase the project is in, the evaluated completion date, and anything that is of general intrigue. Recollect that workers outside of the characterized group may give extra important information and, regardless of whether that doesn't occur, they need incessant and explicit communication to assist them with getting tied up with Lean Six Sigma.

Training

The preparation program should incorporate all business employees, from top management through the Belts and specialists, improvement colleagues, the organization everywhere, and suppliers and clients. Where training frameworks as of now exist, for example, a training organization or only a preparation database, the training on Lean Six Sigma ought to be coordinated into those equivalent frameworks. Your organization will likewise need to conclude whether to affirm its Belts and specialists officially, and assuming this is the case, how to do this.

The executives training should give leaders and chiefs a wise and consolidated introduction to Lean Six Sigma standards, the benefits and costs the organization envisions, and a guide for full usage. For top administrators, this training can be practiced in half day, yet it should be done before all other training. For those leaders who will be involved directly with the usage or project surveys (once in a while called Champions), two days of training is commonly suitable. The extra preparing time will permit these leaders to completely participate in the key parts of Lean Six Sigma and help realize the ideal social changes through exhibiting Lean Six Sigma support in regular basic leadership.

At long last, the organization will require an introduction to Lean Six Sigma. There should be an expectation to go through around two hours portraying the desires for implementation and the roles every employee may have in it. While this may seem like a ton of time spent for the whole organization, it offers you the chance to plant the seeds for the social change that really will include everybody.

Build Teaming and Employee Involvement Culture

This one is obvious. There are different sides to this incentive. This sort of culture is described by "strengthening," which signifies "parting with power." Management must be eager to surrender power on the grounds that there is a degree of trust in their people's ability to perform. Individuals must be given the right instruction and aptitudes to acknowledge power. They likewise need to act capably with that new power and have the position to go about as procedure proprietors. They should approach data and input so they can quantify progress. Organization have made considerable progress with joining and representative contribution, however there are as yet numerous undiscovered open doors right now.

Organizations need to develop workers who are eager to go past their typical activity desires. Albeit most organizations are engaged with teaming and worker contribution at some level, there are a couple of regular predicaments with the teaming mechanics. At times, the ideal individuals who can have a major effect are not engaged with the correct places or they are spread excessively far across groups. Another quandary is the starting of groups and assignments before there is a strong improvement plan. This isn't legitimately a teaming issue; however the point here is that we need to give it our best shot to set the team for success.

About teaming, this is a final thought; Should participation be mandatory? We have had incredible achievement setting up the benchmark that the requirement for the association to change is obligatory and the requirement for workers who are eager to assist execute with changing is compulsory. There is urge for productive member of society workers to set the model for other people. In the end, different workers get the message by means of friend pressure and watching many victories and fall in. Some may never participate and fall to pieces their professions.

Implement Regulated Program Management

One of the missteps administrators make with Six Sigma and other improvement programs is to permit the push to escape from them. Left without a well-characterized technique, program management, and performance feedback, these endeavors can take on their very own existence. The primary thing you know, there is a multiplication of groups contained assets that don't have the opportunity to serve on

everyone of them, there are numerous repetitive as well as nonvalue-adding exercises, and very little to appear for it all in the final analysis. Six Sigma is just on a par with the technique, sending, and execution process. Independent from anyone else, it is only an organized critical thinking and problem-solving process, Minitab programming, and a menu of statistical instruments. Prior forms of Six Sigma during the 1980s were only that — a group of measurable savvy people with a sack of apparatuses going around the organization searching for an issue. They blurred away rapidly.

There is a need in organizations for structure and control around Six Sigma to guarantee arrangement among technique and effort. As far as we can tell, organizations starting Six Sigma have a restricted limit level where they can seek after improvements and keep up every day business necessities. Further, it bodes well to focus constrained resources and time on the most elevated impact opportunities. A considerable lot of our customers have a conventional administration procedure to control tasks and movement and measure ROIs project by project. An organized task closeout process can be seen it some, including a high level of custom to project completion and results.

Manage Controversy and Confrontation

Organizations that are not encountering tension and debate with change are having a ton of fun and, truth be told, are most likely not changing by any means. Major key improvement makes a great deal of emotion. We have to expel all the emotions and do a job of overseeing change with data, facts, and analysis. Managing controversy and confrontation in a correct manner, can be healthy when overseen accurately Six Sigma for Small and Mid-Sized Organizations and in an auspicious way. At the point when an organization starts its improvement venture, there is no response to a large number of these issues. That is the test of improvement. Extraordinary pioneers have a belief, faith diligence, confidence, and certainty that the organization will make sense of how to assemble everything and succeed together.

Encounter is somewhat more grounded. At the point when a competitor's task suggestions are right, bolstered by realities, and upheld by the larger part, at that point associations need to perceive and thump down the obstructions and evacuate the divas. Inability to do this sends a solid message that it is alright not to change, straightforward. Nothing undermines a significant change process more than permitting the nay-sayers to work against the tide of progress.

A few people will never get it regardless of what you do; it isn't in their mind to change or to be a piece of a Six Sigma or group improvement effort. Now and again, there is a spot in the organization for these people, and in some cases the lights go on and these people develop to be your heroes. Sometimes, a portion of these people become threatening and endeavor to undermine and disrupt change. At the point when organization experience this circumstance, looking the other way isn't the appropriate response. You can't pretend that awful execution is acceptable exhibition. Initiative gets organizations through these boundaries and sends a message to the remainder of the organization. Inability to manage improper conduct wrecks responsibility and backing.

Make Proper Investment in Resources

This is a typical hindrance for some associations seeking after Six Sigma. To begin with, individuals must be given new skills through adequate trainings and their required Six Sigma projects. Second, duty of resources is estimated by activities, not words. It is significantly simpler to gripe about designating resources than overseeing them, however effective organizations refuse to compromise on this subject. If you have Six Sigma applicants and their administrators are not permitting time for training and undertaking work, the time has come to intervene, take action and reset the expectation. Something else, an inappropriate message is sent to the remainder of the organization. When resources are focused on a Six Sigma exertion, investment is never again a decision. Try not to let directors pull off compromising that their subordinate's support in Six Sigma implies something different won't complete. Try not to be tricked by the calls of "They don't have the opportunity to do Six Sigma and their normal employment." There is a major distinction between overseeing proactively and directing the manner in which things have consistently been finished. Manage the realities and oversee it! There are consistently alternatives for fitting everything in, except it requires escaping similar individuals, same procedure, same reasoning, same outcomes schedule.

A profound jump into what managers have their people doing is regularly disputable in light of the fact that it doubts the worth include of current action versus improvement action. For these individuals, their measurements are generally made up on the spot to legitimize their activities. Most cases can without much of a stretch be balanced with realities, for example, value-add proportions, dollarizing lost chances, and Cost of Poor Quality. The point here is that once the dedication is made, there is no turning around. You are in, and you will finish that $150,000 cost-decrease venture. Also, the executives will make the earth for progress, not nonparticipation and reasons. Will a cataclysmic client occasion at any point come up in the center of green belt preparing? Without a doubt, however the vast majority of these things can be taken care of. One of the assignments of initiative right now to free the organization of paired reasoning — "In the event that I do An, I can't do B" — and get individuals thoroughly c

COMMON CONCERN ABOUT IMPLEMENTING THE LEAN SIX SIGMA IN YOUR BUSINESS

Fear of Change

You might want to improve the way your business functions. This makes quite a lot of sense. You will need to roll out certain changes, some of them major. It is a fact that numerous individuals fear change. While we may feel good doing likewise things consistently, this implies we will simply continue committing similar errors again and again. At the end of the day, in case you're not ready to change how you do a few things in your business, you won't have the option to improve your business.

Fear of Commitment

Once more, this is a typical issue for some individuals. The facts demonstrate that to arrive at the increases that Six Sigma can create, you must be devoted to it. At the danger of seeming cliché, anything worth having merits working for, isn't that so? You've without a doubt been incredibly dedicated to the achievement of your business. Six Sigma requires a significant level of responsibility, too.

Fear of Disruption

Things may not be going just as you'd like business-wise, yet in any event, it works! At the end of the day, why fix it if it ain't broke (or if nothing else totally broken)? All things considered, your business might be doing fine and dandy, however it can improve. You can make your clients more joyful, you can deliver a superior item or services, you can decrease expenses, and you can make higher profits!

Increased Cost

"Six Sigma implementation or any new program is going to cost me cash and I don't know it will worth the expense". This is a sensible concern, however if you do it appropriately, you can be certain that you will diminish, not increase, your expenses.

Wasted Time Without Results. Perhaps you've attempted different projects to make your tasks progressively proficient and sooner or later these simply didn't work. This is legitimate; however, this shouldn't be an issue with Six Sigma. It's focused on explicit issues with a particular critical thinking and problem-solving procedure, with the objective of removing that issue forever.

These feelings of trepidation and concerns are substantial. All things considered, nobody loves escaping their customary range of familiarity. Yet, if you realize that you won't have the option to beat these worries, at that point this book isn't for you, nor is Six Sigma. Having elevated standards are the way to everything. As an entrepreneur, you should continually go for more—complaceny is your foe. To prevail with Lean Six Sigma, you should be devoted to it. In any case, that won't really be so difficult once you start to see the outcomes.

EXPECTING YOUR BENEFITS

Early in your usage, most likely soon after your first basic training, getting everyone pondering on process improvement simultaneously will cause a torrential slide of simple thoughts. This 'ground natural product' is anything but difficult to get and profit by. Indeed, your organization will be adequately prepared in thorough methodologies, project groups will be amassed, gatherings and reviews will follow, etc. The entirety of this structure is imperative to find a 'higher fruit' up the tree of success. In any case, it is essential to get the simple upgrades immediately. In the event that the improvement is well thought out, proceed and do what needs to be done! Nothing could be a surer passing toll than your organization seeing lean and Six Sigma to be bureaucratic activities of experiencing motions before any genuine comprehension and experience is acquired.

Ensure you go for the quick successes to show the achievement that can be increased through lean and Six Sigma. The degree and size of your underlying projects should be deliberately defined to be both significant and feasible in a generally brief timeframe. At that point ensure you generally celebrate and communicate the outcomes and awards as a model for all and more good things to come. If your organization is regular, you'll see some quick upgrades. Progressively generous upgrades will likely require the principal wave of new projects to be finished in two to four months, trailed by extra projects.

CHAPTER FOUR:
LEAN SIX SIGMA TOOLS AND TECHNIQUES TO MANAGE YOUR BUSINESS

Lean Six Sigma and its instruments have made tremendous impact in the activities of numerous organizations. Lean and Six Sigma tools can be used to advance improvement in quality both as a deliberate and strategic way. The vast majority of the instructed Lean Six Sigma techniques or tools are quality methods that are not so much new. What can be distinctive is just the application and combination of the instruments. As an information driven strategy, Lean Six Sigma utilizes tools and techniques which are precise to identify difficulties, take care of issues, and achieve business objectives.

A considerable lot of these tools and techniques were being used some time before the Lean Six Sigma philosophy was detailed, and have been initiated into this approach. One of the amazing parts of Lean Six Sigma is that numerous tools are accessible for use in each stage. A group would then be able to pick the techniques or tools that best accommodates their circumstance. Organizations will frequently have a most loved arrangement of methods dependent on their corporate culture or historical inclinations.

Lean Six Sigma tools are remembered for its Define-Measure-Analyze-Improve-Control (DMAIC) improvement projects execution guide. This current guide's execution is to make processes robust in nature, that let organizations achieve some level of standards that are high and in charge. In Lean Six Sigma, information is exposed to analysis so as to get an understanding of issues and get the needs of clients identified. The Lean Six Sigma phases are to evaluate potential defects and its causes, alongside the decrease of waste from process.

These tools and techniques are sorted out depending on the kinds of investigation in which they are utilized. A significant number of these could be utilized in various phrases of a Lean Six Sigma project and this is contingent on the problem and analysis being done.

Process analysis tools and techniques

The tools and techniques are associated, often with lean portion of the analysis. Procedure examination devices and strategies are regularly connected with the Lean part of the investigation. Depicting the process and getting a clear picture on its proficiency, is what they help to do.

Process Map – a graphical presentation that shows the connections between all process steps and choices focuses inside a procedure. Each progression is a different thing on the procedure map. The Business process mapping is an approach to imagine the business procedure and better see how it functions. A regular guide or map helps to plots the responsibilities and obligations, and also norms associated with the process. It displays this information in an organized manner that shows the means of the process alongside who is capable, what the sources of info and outputs are, and other data applicable to the procedure

Business process mapping is an extraordinary guide in critical thinking as well as problem solving. The whole process can be visualized with this, making it simpler to perceive anything wrong and get directly to the cause of the problem. It likewise assists with envisioning the people and their roles within the process and guarantee everybody have idea on what to do. Notwithstanding that, business process mapping is extraordinary for finding the potential dangers the process makes. Developing a guide in the form of a map makes you reexamine each steps or progression of the procedure and check whether there are any liabilities hidden.

Flow: Flow is the dynamic accomplishment of assignments along the value stream so an item continues from its design to when launched, order to delivery and crude to completed materials in the hands of the client without any stoppages, scrap, or reverses. It is the most widely recognized sort of a process map. While this map is less adaptable, you can without much of a stretch draw it by hand or in programming like MS Office. Flowcharts are regularly utilized for the production of work process charts.

Value Stream Map – a unique instance of a process map that shows the essential move through a process when each progression goes as arranged. It is the arrangement of steps that help create the client value from the process. The value stream map shows a representation of the data and materials required to carry the item to a client. This instrument is useful for streamlining the generation procedure. Despite the fact that value stream mapping is fundamentally utilized in lean manufacturing, it tends to be valuable for businesses or organizations in practically any industry. Its principle objective is to see such data as timeframe, error rate, and superfluous deferrals inside the procedure.

Value stream map comprises of three distinct parts: the procedure map, the course of events, and the data stream. It utilizes an extraordinary arrangement of images to assist you with bettering comprehend the procedure. The procedure map incorporates every one of the means associated with the business procedure. The timetable originates from the procedure map and condenses all the information on term of the procedure. The data stream clarifies how every one of these means collaborates with one another.

There are 3 things value stream mapping encourages you distinguish:

Value-enabling activities

Value-adding activities

Non-value adding activities

The entire motivation behind this map or guide is to kill the entirety of your activities which are Non-value adding and eliminating hold up times between steps in your processes to become progressively minimized, exact, and quick.

As-Is Process – this the procedure guide or value stream map that shows all the means in the process as it is really happening in the present business condition. This isn't really equivalent to what is archived in the techniques. Value Stream Mapping (VSM) is a pencil and paper apparatus utilized in two phases. At first, follow an item's production way from start to finish and create a visual portrayal of each procedure in the material and data streams. Second, draw a future state guide of how value should flow. The most significant guide is the future state map.

To-Be Process – this is the ideal procedure guide or value stream map after the solution of the problem has been executed. This is regularly reflected in amended procedure documentation that is discharged as a component of the implementation.

Data Boxes – these are boxes on a process guide or value stream map that are related with each progression. The data box is utilized to record the measurements related with that progression in the process, for example, process duration, value included time, output, stock, or assets.

TAKT Time – this is a period measure related with the procedure. It mirrors the measure of time that is allocated for each procedure step that guarantees the procedure can satisfy the client need. Takt Time alludes to the rate at which a completed item is finished to fulfill client need. It is a basic tool for recognizing if products are moving from each station to the following in a proficient way, guaranteeing that you can satisfy client need.

In German, 'Takt' lives in the lexical field of time and cadence. In that sense, 'Takt' is the cadenced beat of your organization, and like a music conductor, Takt

Time is intended to give you the way to gauge procedures to guarantee persistent flow and the ideal use of machines and procedures.

Takt Time is adequately your sell rate and is a decent estimation of how proficient your work forms are. In a perfect world, an ideal organization ought to have the capacity that can undoubtedly fulfill need without having a lot of stock in inventory. Used adequately, Takt Time can Promote effectiveness. Your organization will have the option to quantify waste and effectively observe which production areas are struggling, on plan, and in any case should be balanced

Value Added Time – this is the bit of time allowed for processing within a stage where a component of client value is being made on a solitary item or product coursing through the procedure. The worth included time is typically a low level of complete time inside a stage, and is zero for some means.

Move Throughput Yield – this is a computation of the probability that a thing will go through each progression in the process being effectively handled on the primary pass through that progression. It is determined by multiplying all the progression yield value from a worth stream map.

Work-cells – this is a procedure structure that is regularly used to accelerate course through the procedure. All procedure steps are orchestrated together in a work cell which decreases time squandered in handoffs between steps.

Kanban – this is a visual booking approach utilized in management of process where a stage gives a sign to the stage preceeding it thereby indicating that it is prepared for the following item. This methodology limits stock and guarantees each step is dealing with the item that is now generally significant for that step to process. At the point when you shop at a general store, you don't stock up for month or years ahead. Neither does the store stock things that it doesn't hope to sell at the present time. Rather, you tailor your shopping rundown to what you need at the present time, much the same as the store bases its stockpile of the items on client request. Kanban mirrors this course of action by permitting the interest for the company's yield to control the stock of its stock.

Kanban framework sets limits for the stock holding for all present business forms. This liberates extra assets and permits to utilize them better. Kanban framework deals with a straightforward and exquisite thought: possibly enact the inventory network when the interest requires it. This framework both carries more concentration to the business procedure itself and builds its proficiency.

Advantages of a Kanban pull framework

More capital – less cash will be put resources into extra room for stock

Expanded market dynamism – Whether it is force of the market that influence scalability or a part of the item itself, it tends to be harming to have stock comprising of un-sellable items.

Less work in progress (WIP)

Improved production environment – Kanban gives visual impact and can advance objectives and discerning conversation among colleagues

Simple observing – All colleagues will have a steady input of execution through a breakdown of each phase from beginning to end.

Visual Control – this is a lot of flagging methodologies

that permits administrators to see where procedure bottlenecks are happening and to aid the activities to assuage those bottlenecks. This considers ongoing procedure the executives.

Visual Analysis Tool investigation instruments and strategies

Visual investigation tools and resources are utilized with for all intents and purposes each critical thinking philosophy. These systems can be utilized in numerous stages. Their worth is that they are brisk and straightforward. They are likewise brilliant correspondence strategies with senior administration and the tasks or associations that will be influenced by the arrangement.

Histogram – this is a vertical bar outline that shows the overall size of various classifications of examples or events. It is utilized to recognize what properties are the biggest supporters of a particular occurrence or event. The histogram can be utilized to gain knowledge with respect to how a process reaction identifies with client desires; e.g., existing details or focused on targets, for example, on-time delivery. This instrument can likewise help address the topic of whether the procedure being used can really give an attractive reaction with the goal that client necessities can reliably be met. One preferred position of histogram is that this visual introduction or rundown can frequently be seen even with a look.

Pareto Chart – this is extraordinary version of the histogram. It is in such a way that the largest category is first, the next one is the second largest biggest and proceeds to the littlest classification. A good focus on improvement is provided. If that gives center to progress. Additionally, it is a realistic portrayal of the Pareto Principle: 20 percent of info produces 80 percent of output in some random circumstance. The outline joins a vertical reference diagram and a line chart. The visual chart speaks to the measurements of different business process segments, requested from the biggest to the littlest one. The line diagram speaks to the combined aggregate of these measurements.

Pareto Chart is a tool that picture what part of the process have great impact on output the most. To make such graph, you first make sense of the parts of the process and how to gauge them. When you've done that, you can place this information into a Pareto Chart. This will assist you with perceiving how enormous of an impact on the result every part has. Notwithstanding that, it will give you an idea which is clear and of what requires your prompt consideration.

The y-axis shows a representation of cumulative percentage and a defect frequency, while the x-axis represents response variables as a group. They are displayed as bars. This graph is frequently praised as one of the most significant tools in the Lean Six Sigma tool compartment for helping groups reveal the 20% of sources

Fishbone (Cause and Effect or Ishikawa) Diagram – this is a graphical delineation of all the potential reasons for the issue, sorted out into consistent classes. This turns into a guide for examination to figure out which of the causes adds to the issue. It's one of the most acclaimed six sigma apparatuses, as it permits you to conceptualize different reasons for an issue.

A fishbone outline is an organized tool for conceptualizing. This diagram of cause-and-effect methodology is made to help hierarchical groups recognize potential reasons for a depicted issue. A few people allude to this tool as "Ishikawa" diagram, named after the person who had it designed. The name fishbone starts from the chart's fishbone appearance.

With a fishbone conceptualizing approach, the session is directed around classifications of causes, for example, Methods, People, Machines, Equipment, Materials, Environment and Management. To begin the, the group should express the issue. This announcement is then trailed by conceptualizing for main drivers to the issue around the picked classes.

After the group agrees on the issue articulation, the inquiry is set at the leader of the fishbone. The essential bones of the fish are made out of attracted lines associated with the announcement of the issue. Every one of the principle bones in the fish address one of the picked conceptualizing classifications. Things from the meeting to generate new ideas will be reported as lines associated with these primary bones.

The initial phase in playing out the investigation is to recognize the issue you need to understand. You need to record who chips away at the procedure and when and where the procedure happens. Following stage is to compose the issue in a container on the left-hand side of the paper. At that point you draw an even line stretching out to the opposite finish of the paper. From that point, you draw vertical lines stretching out off of the "spine". On these lines, you compose the significant purposes for the issue and thoroughly consider any potential causes. You can additionally separate these causes into sub-characterizations. When you complete the chart with every single imaginable reason for the issue, you can break down your outcomes. The outcomes may require further testing and examination.

Dissipate Diagram – this is a plot of two qualities related with every datum point. One quality is appeared on the vertical pivot and one on the level hub. The plot will uncover whether there is relationship between's the two characteristics.

Box Plots – this chart shows the spread of information for a parameter and the idea of any focal propensity. The middle portion of the information focuses are appeared in a case with a line at the estimation of the midpoint in the crate. The external portion of the information is part into the upper and lower bits and shows the boundaries and generally information spread.

Run Chart – this is an outline of the consecutive qualities for a parameter as a process is working. The qualities are either each progressive item or result or they are values gathered at set occasions during process activity.

Pie Chart – this is a graph that shows the overall size of classifications of a parameter. They are appeared as cuts of a "pie" speaking to their rate. It is regularly utilized for "previously" and "after" correlations.

Check Sheets – this is a chart demonstrating what is to be estimated on an item, process or administration. It will frequently incorporate the estimation procedure.

Quality Function Deployment (QFD) – this strategy is an outline of how the organized client needs are conveyed across item and procedure parameters. It is frequently used to set execution objectives and recognized both botched chances and squandered movement.

Solution Selection Matrix – this instrument is a framework that thinks about solution alternatives over a few criteria. At the point when done utilizing in addition to and short images, it turns into a Pugh Concept Generation Matrix. The other alternative is to allot scores to every choice and loads to the criteria. The framework would then be able to be utilized to assess the alternatives to choose the one with the most noteworthy score.

Bottlenecks – these are zones in a procedure map with tangled stream or steps where stock amasses. Bottlenecks are gatherers of waste. There is a waste related with moderate moving stock and waste related with the additional administration expected to oblige the bottleneck.

Poka Yoke – this is a lot of orders that epitomize the guideline of blunder sealing. Through the plan of the item or procedure, checks are inserted to keep botches from being made or to make them quickly evident so they can be fixed. Named after the Japanese expressions for "blunder" and "machine administrator," poka-burden alludes to any instrument in a procedure that lessens the recurrence of errors, with a definitive objective of empowering individuals and procedures to get things right the first run through. Poka burden can be applied to most procedures, however regions where it can demonstrate fundamental incorporate occurrences while certain procedure has been recognized which brings about continuous human blunder, in circumstances where the client can make a mistake, when a minor blunder transforms into a significant blunder, or when anytime where a blunder will prompt significant disturbance.

Advantages of Poka burden

There is promotion of responsibility and process improvement

Moderately low exertion and not very tedious and time consuming

Ensures that legitimate conditions exist before the real creation, and keeps abandons from occurring.

Distinguishes and disposes of reasons for interruption or disruption

Poka Yoke is an extraordinary method for halting mistakes from developing in any way before they become greater issues.

Kaizen (Continuous Improvement)- The Kaizen procedure is a ground-breaking methodology that powers a nonstop motor for business improvement. It involves the practice of persistently observing, distinguishing, and executing improvements. This is an especially valuable practice for the assembling segment. A decrease in waste is ensured by collective and ongoing improvements, and also, just as quick change at whatever point the littlest wastefulness is watched. Kaizen guarantees that waste will be step by step decreased through the aggregate gifts and information on everybody in the organization cooperating to change the littlest wasteful aspects day by day.

Five "S" Disciplines – these are a lot of working environment organization teaches that are visual in nature and give a sign of whether the work environment is going on smoothly with its operations. Deployment of the Five "S" Disciplines improves quality and employee wellbeing and confidence. The Five S's of lean is a procedure that shows good outcomes in a work environment that is spotless, uncluttered, safe, and efficient to help decrease any form of waste and enhance profitability. It's intended to help build up a quality workplace, both genuinely and intellectually. The 5S way of thinking applies in any work region appropriate for visual control and lean creation. The system includes completing 5 things that all beginning with S in both English and Japanese. They comprise of seiri (sort), seiton (set), seiso (sparkle), seiketsu (institutionalize), and shitsuke (continue). The motivation behind 5S is to make a work environment better by making it a simpler work environment. This happens by seeming well and good; materials and tools are set in legitimate areas dependent on who needs them, how every now and again they're required, and so on. Spaces are cleaned routinely. Cleaning and association become propensities. At the point when utilized effectively, 5S at last makes forms more secure and progressively productive.

> Seiri (Sort) – Remove every single pointless thing for your present generation, leaving just what is vital. This progression centers around the disposal of any superfluous work environment mess. In a procedure called "red labeling," all work environment things are figured out, with a red label put on any that are not completely vital for finishing an undertaking. When tools, supplies, materials and gear have been labeled,

they are then moved to a holding zone for a subsequent assessment. Things that are used in a seldom manner can be put away nearer in vicinity to the workspace, while old mess ought to be disposed of.

Seiton (Set In Order) – Organize remaining things and mark or give them labels in like manner. The objective of this progression is to inspect strategies for capacity that are powerful and proficient, in some cases alluded to as "visual administration," and afterward make a workplace that is composed, ergonomic, uncluttered and effectively traversable. A few inquiries to pose during this progression may be: Which explicit things are expected to play out an assignment? What number of things should be promptly open and where would it be a good idea for them to be found?

The deliberate stockpiling of materials implies that each thing has a foreordained area where it will stay until it utilized, and afterward it will be returned promptly following its utilization. Giving labels and shading coding are additionally useful strategies to use right now. With a sorted out and proficient utilization of capacity, everybody is effectively ready to find significant things and appreciate a less distressing workplace.

Seiso (Shine) – Clean and assess your work zone and everything in it consistently. With the messiness gone and the capacity composed, the subsequent stage is to appropriately and altogether clean the work region consistently. This progression is basic as a method for supporting the improvements started in the Sort and Set stages. All stockpiling regions, machines, gear, devices and work surfaces must be cleaned and checked routinely. Representatives will feel increasingly great right now uncluttered condition, which could likewise prompt expanded responsibility for association's objectives and vision.

Seiketsu (Standardize) – Write out your measures for the Sort, Set In Order, and Shine ventures above. Since the initial three stages are in play, it's an ideal opportunity to institutionalize these new practices. All representatives should be remembered for the formation of a lot of measures that will end up being the new standard for the workspace. At the point when these new models and best practices are executed, the old propensities will before long cease to exist and be supplanted by the more productive examples of conduct. New measures, nonetheless, will most likely require some oversight and implementation until they are routine; updates, for example, visuals and messages are powerful devices to enable these new guidelines to get unchangeable.

Shitsuke (Sustain) – Apply the benchmarks you've set for your organization and make them propensities for everybody in your association. This is surely the most testing: staying sufficiently restrained to support the positive changes made in the initial three stages. It is important that the new framework be kept up or the endeavors and costs put into building up the new framework will be inconsequential. By setting up a conventional framework that incorporates normal preparing and correspondence, representatives will have the option to serenely fit in with the organization's 5S methodology.

Single-Minute Exchange of Die (SMED) - A technique related with lean assembling that decreases the time it takes to run the present item to run the following. It is utilized to quicken process duration, lessen expenses, and improve the flexibility of procedures. Likewise called Quick Changeover.

Advantages of SMED:

Less personal time and improved responsiveness to clients.

WIP and part size decrease.

Improved machine/asset usage.

By expanding the quantity of changeovers, we can convey less stock of crude materials, supplies and completed products.

Become increasingly effective and search for opportunities for nonstop improvement

Total Productive Maintenance (TPM) - a strategy for keeping up and improving the nature of frameworks, procedures, and machines. TPM explicitly expects to lessen loses that are brought about when spontaneous personal time happens.

Statistical analysis tools and techniques

The statistical analysis, techniques and tools are regularly connected with the Six Sigma part of the examination. These tools help us to understand the information and to figure out what is critical and what isn't. The utilization of measurable programming, for example, Excel Analysis Tool Pak or the Minitab application has limited the measure of scientific calculation that the colleagues must do. In any case, they despite everything need to comprehend which measurable methods to use in every circumstance and how to decipher the outcomes.

Procedure Capability – this is a factual proportion that contrasts the ordinary procedure inconstancy and the client or determination limits. It is communicated with process ability lists of Cp, Pp, Cpk, Ppk, or procedure sigma. The capability ratio of a process is an incredible indicator of whether the procedure will have the option to produce outcomes that are defects tree.

Descriptive Statistics – these are statistics that portray the typical conduct of a deliberate parameter within a procedure or item. It incorporates the mean, middle, mode, and standard deviation.

Inferential Statistics – these are statistics used to relate the factual presentation of an example to the measurable execution of the bigger information populace that the example speaks to. These insights depend on the examining approach utilized and incorporate certainty interim and certainty level.

Estimation System Analysis – this is a far-reaching investigation of an examination or test frameworks capacity to effectively decide a deliberate an incentive inside a procedure or item. It incorporates an evaluation of exactness, accuracy, steadiness, linearity, and segregation.

Gage R&R – this is a subset of a measurement system analysis that have focus on the accuracy of the estimation framework. It is a lot of analyses utilizing items or procedures with foreordained known qualities and estimating them to decide if the estimations framework will reliably allocate similar qualities.

Hypothesis Tests – These are statistical data tests which help to decide if a assumption made about the data or information can be confirmed or not. Ordinarily, it is utilized within Lean Six Sigma to decide whether information tests are comparable or if there is a measurable contrast. If that informational indexes can be demonstrated to be disparate, that means that the factor which isolates the two informational indexes significantly affects procedure or item execution. There are various measurable systems utilized relying on whether the information is typical or non-ordinary, continuous or discrete, and the quantity of informational collections or parameters being assessed.

Correlation – this is a test of hypothesis that is utilized to show whether two continuous information parameters are related, and how they are related.

Regression Tests – this is a speculation test that decides the scientific connection between two or more continuous parameters of data.

T Tests – this group of tests of hypothesis which is utilized to show comparison between the descriptive statistics of two datv samples or more to decide whether they are comparable.

ANOVA – this system is utilized to think about the graphic measurements of at least two information tests to decide whether they are comparative.

Test of Proportions – this group of speculation tests is utilized to decide whether two examples of discrete information are comparative.

Chi-Square Test – this method is utilized to decide whether at least two examples of discrete information are comparative.

Design of Experiments – this is a measurable system for making a lot of tests with test examples that are intended to incorporate or avoid certain features and with qualities set at the base or greatest level. In view of the arrangement of tests, a best-case configuration can be made with the proper structure highlights and configuration targets. This strategy is frequently utilized when making another item or procedure during the Improve stage.

Control Charts – these are diagrams that track the presentation of chose procedure or item parameters and decides if the variety that is shown is because of normal causes or exceptional causes. There are various control diagram plans, in light of the qualities of the information and the characteristic being estimated. These graphs are ordinarily utilized in the Control stage as methods for guaranteeing the improved procedure execution is continued.

Project and team management tools and techniques

Lean Six Sigma projects should likewise have the option to associate with partners and clients. There are a few methods that have demonstrated compelling right now. A portion of these depend on understanding the point of view of outer partners and a portion of these are valuable for sorting out and speaking with interior partners, for example, colleagues.

Critical to Quality (CTQ) – these are the process, item, or service parameters that are the characteristics of client value. They are dictated by the partners, not the project group.

Project Charter – this is a project management report used to approve the given project and give limits on the extent of the action. From various organizations to others, this format varies. It works both as the outline for the business procedure and as lawful approval of the task. Project Charter for the most part, incorporates the overview of the project, it's scope, insights regarding the group and the assets, and the timetable. It gives all of you the fundamental data about the task and explains the central matters about it.

The fundamental advantage of a Project Charter is that it keeps things less disorganized. When a group jumps into the task, it is anything but difficult to forget about who is liable for what, which cutoff times the group needs to meet first, and so on. In the event that the organization doesn't have a reasonable administrative progression, things will get considerably messier.

Having a task Project Charter encourages you to maintain a reasonable spotlight on what your venture is about. It lets you comprehend the task's structure and the connection between the individuals in question. As it were, Project Charter encourages you take your firm back to its usual state of orderliness when things get confounding.

In-frame/Out-of-frame – this system is utilized to explain limits for a project group. The extent of the task is depicted in the frames. Areas that are not to be remembered for the analysis are recorded as out-of-outline.

SIPOC – This represents Supplier, Input, Process, Output, Customer. It is a method used to characterize the points of confinement of the process that is being examined and to explain the partners for the procedure. It centers around the fundamentals of the process and the individuals in question. By stripping all additional data, it characterizes a complex venture better as far as its essential components.

Cross-functional team– this alludes to what the Lean Six Sigma group is made up of. Typically, there is at any rate one delegate from each function who has obligation regarding performing activities within the procedure being examined.

Team decision making – this is a lot of practices utilized by groups to arrive at agreement when deciding. Although, most of the conclusions of the team are dictated by the data analysis results, there are still choices to be made in group activity, solution improvement, and planning of implementation.

Stakeholder management – this is a lot of practices that are utilized to distinguish the key partners for the Lean Six Sigma venture. The key performance goals and communication design are additionally settled for every partner.

Culture change management – this is a set of communication and implementation activities that is centered on building purchase in and support for changing processes and work rehearses. This is regularly required during the Improve and Control stages to guarantee the solution is suitable and feasible.

Implementation planning – the execution of the solution is frequently a task as large or greater than the Lean Six Sigma project analysis. This is a lot of practices relating to project management used to design and execute a task.

RACI matrix - Responsibility Assignment Matrix, otherwise called RACI network, is a table that depicts the obligations of each colleague on each errand of the business process. RACI represents Responsible, Accountable, Consulted, and Informed – the key duties most regularly utilized in the framework.

Responsible refers to those whose job is to accomplish the undertaking. Also, it refers to is the individual appointing the assignments to other people and checking how they progress. There is in every case just one responsible per task. Counseled are the specialists on the topic whose suppositions control those taking a shot at the task.

Ordinarily, RACI matrix has the errands indicated on the left of the table and the colleagues recorded in the top line. The cells at the convergence of the two have the letter relating to what the individual handles inside the errand. This straightforward framework helps each colleague plainly comprehend their job all the while. It likewise permits you to see the holes in the group structure and which jobs you need to fill.

Other tools and techniques include:

Failure Mode and Effects Analysis (FMEA) - A model that assists experts with breaking down and organize shortcomings and potential imperfections of a structure or process dependent on factors which include severity and recurrence of event.

Created during the 1950s, FMEA is utilized to survey segments, gatherings, and subsystems to recognize failure modes and their circumstances and end results. Lean Six Sigma experts use FMEA to improve the nature of their procedures, services, and items by identifying and fixing issues before they happen.

Visual working environment: A visual work environment is characterized by gadgets intended to outwardly share data about hierarchical tasks so as to make human and machine execution more secure, progressively definite, increasingly repeatable, and progressively solid.

Voice of the client: Quality capacity organization (QFD) starts with an investigation and revelation of client needs. The initial step is to catch the voice of the client (VOC) and afterward make a voice of the client table (VOCT). The method is planned for giving the client the best items and services. It catches the changing needs of the client through immediate and aberrant techniques. The voice of the client system is utilized in the "characterize' period of the DMAIC technique, typically to additionally characterize the issue to be tended to. Regular sources can incorporate deals and specialized outing reports, guarantee claims, client bolster gatherings or help lines, and online networking.

Standard Work - Standard work, it is the documentation of the accepted procedures for any procedure or assignment at that given minute. It is made and refreshed by the individuals who take the necessary steps. It shapes the standard for development and guarantees process consistency.

Gemba Walks-The Japanese word "Gemba" signifies the real place. During a Gemba walk, the manager goes to where work is done to show regard for the representatives, pose inquiries, and possibly recognize opportunities for development.

Hoshin Kanri-Hoshin Kanri (in any case called, Policy Deployment) is a key planning approach intended to adjust the organization and guarantee that everybody is progressing in the direction of similar objectives. The methodology adjusts the need to accomplish day by day steady improvement while pushing toward the association's three to five-year leap forward targets simultaneously.

PDSA-PDSA is an elective improvement cycle that represents Plan, Do, Study, Act. It is a rearranged rendition of DMAIC that works best for development extends that are not overwhelming on measurements.

Problem solving and Improvement

In spite of amazing control, now and then issues will occur, or development opportunities will be distinguished. All things considered, at least one of the accompanying Six Sigma tools can be made use of.

A3 Problem Solving-A3 it is an organized problem solving or critical thinking approach that gets its name from the size of paper that was utilized before advanced instruments like digital tools got accessible. An A3 report is the consequence of an improvement cycle like DAMIC or PDSA.

Catchball-The Six Sigma strategy of Catchball includes passing ideas starting with one individual then onto the next for criticism and activity. The thought or idea (ball) is gotten under way whenever somebody characterizes a test or opportunity. It at that point it moves to and fro, upwards and down, or both until an arrangement is created and settled upon.

Standardized Work - A benchmark idea in kaizen or ceaseless improvement that is utilized as an instrument for keeping efficiency and quality at ideal levels. Standardized work archives the present best practice. At the point when a better than ever framework is embraced, it turns into the new institutionalized work. At its center, it is tied in with guaranteeing your activities run as easily as would be prudent and your procedure improvement technique is continually advancing and being received by your workers.

Standardized work is imperative to arriving at your optimal Takt Time.

Advantages of institutionalized work: - Best practices are followed

Procedure improvement never closes

Lessens waste

Improves scaling endeavors

Makes variations from the norm increasingly noticeable

Less time spent on guesswork

Statistical Process Control (SPC) - A procedure that make use of statistical instruments to screen, control, and improve the nature of processes

Regression Analysis- can be helpful to establish that a procedure input has a relationship to the yield of a procedure. This information can help distinguish a contribution to the process where control is important to accomplish an ideal procedure yield reaction. Potential issues when utilizing relapse investigation include:

• Correlation doesn't suggest causation.

• Multicollinearity can cause destruction in an analysis and endanger the legitimacy of its decisions. Multicollinearity happens when in a relapse model at least two of the indicators are respectably or profoundly corresponded.

• A model probably won't be precise in light of the fact that a couple of extreme data points can give abundance influence that mutilates legitimacy of the model.

You would utilize it to characterize the scientific connection between a output variable (y) and any number of input variables (x1, x2, and so forth.). Taking graph of these data inputs and outputs encourages you picture examples or abnormality from wanted examples in your work process. In carrying out regression analysis, be cautious, Here are a couple of things to recall when playing out a regression analysis:

At the point when two variables are seen as to be correlated, it is enticing to expect that this shows one variable causes the other, bringing about the fallacy of correlation, doesn't suggest causation. At least two factors in your regression model could be exceptionally associated, making it hard to confine their individual consequences for the dependent variable, alluded to as Multicollinearity. At the point when the blunder term in one timespan is emphatically corresponded with the mistake term in the past timeframe, you'll experience the issue of (positive first-request) autocorrelation.

Run Chart/Time Series-A run diagram is fundamentally a chart showing time arrangement data, where the information are sequenced from first to last. This apparatus can show patterns and moves. In any case, care should be practiced since now and again a pattern may give off an impression of being happening however this evident procedure move may just be the consequence of basic reason fluctuation; i.e., changes in a reaction due to not-bizarre clamor

varieties from the procedure.

Root Cause Analysis/The 5 Whys-This method assists with finding problems and the causes associated with them under consideration and this is used in the "analyze" phase of the cycle, DMAIC.

In the 5 Whys system, the inquiry "why" is asked, over and over, at last paving the way profoundly issue. Albeit "five" is a general guideline, the genuine number of inquiries can be more noteworthy or less, whatever it takes to pick up lucidity.

Record the issue you're having so everybody in your group can concentrate on it explicitly.

Inquire as to why the issue happened.

If your first answer isn't the root cause of issue, inquire as to why, once more.

This process should be repeated multiple times to locate the cause of the issue. You can inquire as to why in excess of multiple times, yet it appears that after 5 whys are asked, you will have lucidity on the reason for your concern.

Brainstorming- is the key procedure of any problem solving or critical thinking strategy and is regularly used in the "improve" period of the DMAIC approach. It is an important procedure before anybody begins utilizing any tools. Brainstorming includes skipping thoughts and producing imaginative approaches to move toward an issue through escalated freewheeling discussions in groups.

Benchmarking-Benchmarking is the strategy that utilizes a set standard of estimation. It includes making examinations with different organizations to increase a free evaluation of the given circumstance. Benchmarking may include looking at significant procedures or divisions inside a business (inward benchmarking), contrasting comparative work regions or capacities and industry pioneers (utilitarian benchmarking), or contrasting comparable items and administrations and that of contenders (serious benchmarking).

UTILIZING VISUAL MANAGEMENT

Visual administration takes numerous structures in the working environment and furthermore outside of it; traffic signs are a conspicuous model! In the working environment, an assortment of presentations, graphs, signs, names, colourcoded markings, etc can be used. Utilizing a visual methodology enables everybody to perceive what's happening, comprehend the procedure and realize that undertakings are being completed or things put away effectively. Visual management is a corresponding way to deal with help the Five Ss, the control plan, wellbeing and security, kanban and that's just the beginning. Just as assisting with appearing if something is strange or missing, visual management is likewise used to plainly stamp walkways or stopping zones, or to recognize locales – where a hard cap should be worn, for instance. An unmistakable connect to the Five Ss exists.

Displays and controls could incorporate information or data for the individuals working in a specific zone, keeping them educated regarding in general execution or concentrated on explicit quality issues. Visual controls could likewise cover security, generation throughput, material stream or quality measurements, for instance. Basically, visual administration is a significant procedure for supporting improvement; it guarantees the working environment is efficient and that things can be handily found. It's an exceptionally powerful method for imparting results and including individuals. Visual management isn't sufficient without anyone else, however. It needs to appropriate and opportune activities. The performance of process review meetings are very important.

CHAPTER FIVE: LEAN SIX SIGMA CHAIN OF EVENTS: GETTING THE WORK DONE IN BUSINESS

As a director, your job is to chip away at the processes that you make do in view of progress. You in this manner need to know correctly how these processes work. Having an up-todate image of how things are done makes DMAIC (Define, Measure, Analyze, Improve and Control) improvement extends far simpler to attempt. The Measure period of DMAIC is tied in with seeing how and how well the work gets completed. There's have to see how the work at present completes. Simply after you see how the procedure functions presently would you be able to see the open doors for development in your procedure and oversee execution better.

The most effective method to draw a process map is the primary focal point of this section. We see two sorts: the deployment flowchart and the value stream map. These maps expand on the elevated level SIPOC outline and give extremely supportive pictures of how the work is done. Before you draw any sort of process map, visit the work environment and see with your own eyes what's truly occurring. The Japanese allude to this perception as 'heading off to the Gemba'. 'The Gemba' is a Japanese expression for the 'actual place' ' – that is, the place the activity is. Just in the Gemba can you genuinely perceive how things are done and it's the main spot where genuine improvement can happen. You might have the option to draw up better approaches for taking every necessary step in some focal administration area, or in a building office, however the fact of the matter is the Gemba. That is the place things are characterized, and refined, to deliver real and viable change.

You're probably going to discover shocks sitting tight for you in the Gemba. Frequently you'll discover the procedure is being completed distinctively to how you thought it was occurring, particularly when more than one group is included. Procedures, for example, process stapling and spaghetti graphs are secured. These strategies help you to see the truth of your work environment and empower you to recognize superfluous steps and take out waste.

PRACTICING PROCESS STAPLING

Procedure stapling offers one approach to truly comprehend the procedure and the chain of occasions. Simply, process stapling implies taking a client request, for instance, and truly strolling it through the whole procedure, bit by bit, as if you were the request. Regardless of where the request goes, you go as well. By following the request, you begin to perceive what truly occurs, who does what and why, how, where and when they do it. Completing a procedure stapling exercise with a little group of individuals can be a perfect initial step. Some of the time, there can be preferences in starting the activity from the finish of the procedure and working in reverse. Individuals will be less acquainted with this 'switch stream', helping them ponder things.

You start to see all the means all the while and how much time and development is engaged with completing the work. Procedure stapling causes you distinguish various improvement openings, regardless of whether you don't utilize the activity to make a spaghetti chart or procedure map.

You may, for instance, recognize the degree for cleaning up the working environment, making it simpler and more secure to discover things. The procedure stapling exercise encourages you detect the dissatisfactions all the while, for example, irregularities and why for heaven's sake do-we-do this? exercises. You would then be able to see the means that include placing or developing value and those that don't. It's normal for just 10–15 percent of the means in a process to add value and usually, the 'thing' experiencing the process spends as meager as 1 percent of the absolute process time in these means. While presenting process stapling, you may discover a few people disclosing to you this is the thing that they as of now do. Be that as it may, what they really do is get a gathering of individuals in a room and go through clingy notes to help draw the procedure. They're overlooking what's really important! The image they draw will be what they believe is going on. Process stapling empowers you to perceive what's truly occurring. You can take a stab at making photographs of each stride simultaneously. Aside from giving a perfect record of what you've seen, photographs empower you to make a powerful introduction to the executives of what you've found. Be set up for them to be amazed.

As your comprehension of the procedure builds, you're probably going to discover genuine incentive in working with your clients to stretch out the procedure stapling idea to fuse their exercises with yours. Right now, can turn out how your procedure and its yield connect to your client's procedure, what your client's procedure resembles and how your client utilizes your procedure yields.

Expanding process stapling gives incredible understanding into how you can create enhancements in your procedure that truly increase the value of your client and have an effect that pleasures them. The procedure can likewise prompt joint improvement action with a DMAIC venture being done working together with your client.

DRAWING SPAGHETTI DIAGRAMS

A spaghetti chart gives an image of what's going on in the process as far as development. The outline tracks the development of the thing or things experiencing the procedure, including the progression of data and the individuals completing the work. You can apply the procedure to any working zone, including your office or even your home. You could even utilize a screen shot of a request passage application, for instance, as the "guide" and afterward follow the way of the PC cursor as the specialist rounds out a structure. Spaghetti graphs are not confined to tasks that are genuinely spread out.

Consider the movements you make and the amount of the distance you travel when undertaking assignments, for example, making photocopies, getting your printing or making some tea. The spaghetti graph may hurl some genuine astonishments about how much movement occurs in your organization, including how regularly things go to and fro. This strategy encourages identify waste and gives a visual catalyst to invigorate change in your working environment.

You may as of now have utilized this strategy at home! In the event that you've introduced another kitchen, you'll know the significance of the triangle framed by the sink, cooker and ice chest. You can utilize various shades. However, it have no extraordinary significance , yet you do need to recognize the movement of individuals, materials and data. At the point when you make a spaghetti graph, you might need to utilize a present office plan, for instance demonstrating where the furnishings, gear and force focuses are found. Ensure the arrangement truly is present and that it incorporates every one of extra things, incorporating those cases in the corner that appear to have showed up from no place.

In building up a spaghetti chart you can gauge how far and why individuals are moving. You might have the option to roll out some straightforward improvements to your office design to lessen the separation moved, or even to maintain a strategic distance from it totally. You could even utilize a long chunk of string or a pedometer to assist you with building up a progressively exact outline and better comprehend the development in question. It's acceptable practice to record the complete separation went on the pattern of the graph, at that point do likewise for the better than ever strategy. You at that point have a proportion of the degree of progress made.

At the point when you use process stapling and spaghetti graphs together, you may see the opportunity for a significant decrease in wasted movement and in other nonvalue-included steps as well. Pointless voyaging and movement burn through so much time. Siting the important individuals and hardware together is regularly a moderately basic method for decreasing waste and time for processing.

PAINTING A PICTURE OF THE PROCESS

When attempting to comprehend your processes and how the work gets completed, the expression 'an image paints a thousand words' is unquestionably valid. Right now take a look at two explicit alternatives for painting that image of your process – a deployment flowchart and a value stream map. Regardless of their names, these are both 'process maps', and in general utilize the term 'process map', will be used. At the point when you paint the image of your procedure, remember why you are doing it. Building up the image causes you see how the work completes and the level of unpredictability simultaneously. Your image can feature the internal and external client and supplier connections or 'interfaces', and assist you with deciding the info and in-process measures you need.

You're not painting this specific picture as your personal computer can change specifications, so keep things basic. This image is for you and will assist you with overseeing and improve the procedure. You are drawing a 'current state' picture to perceive how things are done at this point.

A 'future state' map shows how the procedure could be attempted to accomplish a more significant level of execution at some future point. Accomplishing that presentation might be more enthusiastically and could bring about the requirement for a DMAIC venture. At the point when you've drawn and actualized your image of a future state map, it turns into the present state map. In light of consistent improvement, you currently need to build up another future state picture.

Your image can give a valuable system that prompts an entire scope of inquiries: Who are the clients that have desires for the procedure? For what reason is the procedure done? What is its motivation? Does everybody included comprehend the reason? What are the worth included and non-esteem included advances? How might you complete fundamental non-value included steps, utilizing negligible assets? What are the basic achievement factors – that is, the things you should progress admirably? For what reason is the procedure done when it is finished? On the off chance that choices should be made as a feature of the procedure, are the criteria that will be utilized to settle on the choices comprehended by everybody included? Are the choices conveyed satisfactorily? Are as far as possible suitable? How would you and others manage issues that happen simultaneously? What are the most well-known slip-ups that happen all the while? What effect do these errors have on the clients? Where have upgrades previously been attempted simultaneously? What was the result? Whichever addresses you ask, remember to continue asking 'Why?'

KEEPING THINGS SIMPLE

Process mapping utilizes bunches of various images, or 'shows'; attempt to use as not many as could be expected under the circumstances. In making a deployment flowchart, only a few conventions are typically enough: the circle, the square box and the diamond. The circle shows the points for starting and also stopping, in your process. The square box implies a stage or activity. The diamond suggests a conversation starter, where the appropriate response figures out which course the process follows straightaway.

DEVELOPING A DEPLOYMENT FLOWCHART

The Use of deployment flowchart expands on the high level SIPOC graph, and goes into somewhat more detail, however not all that much. This flowchart recognizes who's engaged with the process and what they do, including the various individuals from a group who are associated with various phases of the process, and furthermore different groups and divisions, the internal clients, and suppliers. Spotting moments of truth is simpler when utilizing a deployment flowchart. Moments of truth are contact focuses with the client (when a client comes into contact with an organization)'. Before you start dealing with a deployment flowchart, ensure you have a goal for the procedure that mirrors the CTQs (Critical to Quality). What's more, ensure you can respond to the inquiry, 'For what reason would you say you are doing this process? '

Include the individuals who work the process when you build up an organization flowchart. Since various recognitions exist of how the procedure functions, utilize a clingy note for each progression all the while with the goal that you can move things around just. You may well find that the procedure is more unpredictable than you might suspect it is, which is the reason doing a process stapling exercise initially can be so valuable. At the point when you've utilized your clingy notes to make a flowchart, consider utilizing process mapping programming to officially report the procedure.

These diagrams generally have vertical lines between the various individuals and are regularly alluded to as "swim path" graphs. Each time a flow arrow crosses a separating line, you ought to think about taking an estimation. You have to remember the client for the image to assist you with recognizing the moments of truth. PC frameworks can likewise be remembered for your cast of characters. Work may be contribution to the PC framework, for instance, with the yield turning out elsewhere. Seeing the entire picture is fundamental. at the point when the diagram moves evenly and down, a client and provider relationship exist.

Most issues happen at the interfaces between two individuals or two divisions. Measures are in all likelihood vital here to help screen performance and recognize if problems exist, maybe brought about by not getting a clear picture of the necessities. Your outcomes here, particularly the degree of remodification will majorly affect your performance for the client, so assembling great information and comprehending what's going on is fundamental.

Estimating time can feature other opportunities for improvement. For instance, you may ask to what extent each progression takes and for what valid reason. You're just estimating unit time – the time it makes to finish this stride. While this estimation could incite some fascinating inquiries, seeing the master plan is increasingly useful as it additionally incorporates the passed or process duration. This estimation is the time it takes to finish the whole procedure. (Passed or process duration is at times alluded to as the lead time.)

Working in the process duration or cycle time encourages you to recognize bottlenecks and dead time – alleged on the grounds that from the client's point of view nothing's going on. In your processes, attempt to recognize and oversee bottlenecks, to pose inquiries that explain your comprehension and to consistently search for development openings.

SEEING THE VALUE IN A VALUE STREAM MAP

A value stream map is either an expansion or an option in contrast to the deployment flowchart as a perspective on work gets completed in your organization. The term 'value stream' is a deceptive depiction. The value stream map shows all the tasks both value making and non-valuecreating, which take your item from idea to dispatch, or from request to conveyance, for instance. These activities incorporate strides to process data from the client, and steps to change the item on its way to the client.

Value stream maps follow the product path which is from request to conveyance to decide current conditions, yet they can likewise remember an image of the genuine working design for the workplace or plant to feature the effect of transport time, for instance. You can make and utilize your worth stream map such that works for you.

Preferably, your procedure map incorporates the external client. You have to perceive and comprehend the entire procedure or framework and to detect the snapshots of truth. Procedure stapling is a perfect initial step to assist you with making a worth stream map – and you truly need to go to the Gemba to perceive what's going on.

The value stream map is like the organization of a SIPOC outline. In a perfect world, your worth stream map incorporates an image of where the different exercises occur and shows the progression of the two materials and data. It incorporates some additional data; right now, triangle that recognizes work in progress (the 'I' is for stock) – work standing by to be actioned. Where the 'work in progress' is individuals in a line, the 'stock triangle' shows a 'q' instead of an 'I'. Practically speaking, esteem stream maps are clear, however they'll be somewhat more definite and will utilize a larger number of shows than you use in an organization flowchart.

To draw your worth stream map, work through the following steps:

1. Recognize the process you need to take a gander at, concurring with points of starting and stopping points. Depicting the item or service this procedure is supporting is additionally useful. 2. Set up a little group to do the analysis. The group ought to know about all the means in question, from supplier contribution to external client, so it must incorporate individuals working simultaneously.

3. Go to the Gemba. Go where the activity is and watch what really occurs. Value stream mapping begins in the work environment. 4. Working at a sensibly significant level, draw a procedure guide of the material/item stream in the entire worth stream. A few people want to do this activity beginning

at the client end and working in reverse – rather like procedure stapling backward. Record the means as you go, as opposed to attempting to remember everything. Just as material and item stream, make sure to catch the data stream that makes item or material travel through the procedure.

Distinguish the presentation information you'd prefer to know. Helpful data frequently incorporates movement or unit time, process duration, scrap or modify rates, the quantity of staff/assets, cluster sizes, machine uptime, changeover time, working time, stock and accumulation. 6. Gather the information or data needed for each step. Add the information to your guide in boxes. An emphasis on decreasing changeover time was one of the keys to progress for Toyota in picking up piece of the overall industry over a large number of the Western vehicle makers, where it was alluded to as SMED – single minute exchange of die. (In the production system, the casts and molds are reffered to as die)

Add arrows to show data flows. The value stream map shows data flow just as material flow, independently recognizing whether the data is sent physically or electronically. The worth stream map shows the data stream in the top portion of the guide, with the material stream beneath. 8. Add a general course of events to show the normal process duration for a thing. This course of events shows to what extent the thing spends in the entire procedure. You have to take a gander at the bottlenecks featured by the distinction between the unit and process durations, just as the degrees of work in progress or stock distinguished in the triangles between the means.

For instance, of a value stream map, consider XYZ Company's structure process The process starts with customer service accepting an email or phone request. The item cost is checked utilizing the item value database. Accessibility is checked as far as stock inventory utilizing the stock management system. In the event that stock can't be distributed, the request is passed to the assembling group through the assembling request framework and booked for creation the following day. The conveyance date is resolved, the client is exhorted and the request section records are done with through the customer service management system for orders.

Making use of averages is normally fine, however perceive the risk of midpoints and recollect that the real occasions change either side of the mean – known in the frightening universes of insights and arithmetic as 'variation'.

In the example above, XYZ model, the present state map incorporates a few triangles containing the letter 'I'. These triangles are for the degrees of stock, or work in progress. At the point when you make a worth stream map for one of your procedures, you have to recollect that the guide portrays the present condition of your association – a depiction in time. Regardless of whether individuals in the association feel the stock isn't generally that high or low isn't pertinent; for reasons unknown, the stock is the thing that it is at this moment. So as to have a total perspective on things, you have to consolidate information, for example, action time and process duration, and change after some time. The accompanying case of a worth stream map in a help association exhibits how important the expansion of information becomes. It empowers you to perceive how the work completes, yet additionally how well it completes.

CHAPTER SIX:
SOFTWARE SYSTEMS FOR
SIX SIGMA QUALITY

Six Sigma Software Companies can acquire quality software with subjects from 'examining to quality training'. There are in excess of 34 subjects accessible. There are more than 370 software suppliers for these 34 or more quality subjects. Not all product providers give every one of them, yet many give comparative software programs just in an alternate organization or style of yield. The issue a software client has is choosing which software programs are most appropriate for their particular checking and detailing activity. This is a troublesome inquiry to reply since all product programs under a particular heading make attempt to give the best and adequate service to help their clients. One program may function admirably. With this, they will attempt to sell their different programs dependent on introductory outcomes and the satisfaction of the consumer.

Yet, their potential clients, without really attempting the program, has no clue how easy to understand it will be for them. Likewise, is the program easy to use inside their current software programs. Can they interface and utilize a similar stockpiling unit in each sort of program is a significant fundamental inquiry to consider. Having assessed a few software SPC programs and not being a PC master, search for the best easy to use framework, with a decent book and help segment to reply, in your language, any inquiries or issue that happen when evaluating the program. Additionally, search for information assortment programming that will gather and store information in records, for example, Microsoft Excel or Access programming programmable documents or other collection, arranging, or capacity framework. The information must be useable with the product program you propose to utilize.

A few organizations give software that can be down stacked from the Internet for a set number of days for assessment. Here the assessment of the help framework is truly scrutinized as no manual accompanies the download. If "Help" isn't generally easy to understand, at that point, neither will be the program in various experience. In view of the quantity of organizations looking for great quality and test work force on the Internet, requiring programming quality examination and test builds, the market is blasting. Additionally, as the PC business keeps on developing, the interest for outstanding work force will never lessen.

SIX SIGMA (BUSINESS) ORDER ENTRY SOFTWARE REQUIREMENTS

Client care request section PC framework and information input screens must be easy to use permitting all divisions' simple access to organization data. Staff should frequently, in their day by day work, question the computer information framework utilizing screen names or ID explicit to their utilization and necessities. It is imperative to keep the framework both secure yet additionally available for all staff in the organization to utilize and get data on their activities. For instance, all section, every client will have a distinguishing proof name, alloted client number, ship to addresses (if numerous areas) with regularly unique conveyance dates, and differences in the item requested. A supplier's item is recognized by provider exchange name, number, or an office distinguishing proof code. All faculty supporting the client may demand client and item data for their particular occupation connection zones and it must be open without (frequently spelling explicit or truncated) trouble.

BAR CODE TRACKING

Bar coding is a benefit essential in the assembling activity. Business tasks and item manufacturing requires tracking in " Real Time" of their activities. Item in process and finished products put into stock should be recognized with respect to where their area is in the assembling procedure. The sooner they are recognized on the plant floor and checked into the PC system will it help creation control in finding and knowing where and in what phase of completion are items and procedures. Bar coding on work requests and item names work boxes of material in process, when filtered after explicit tasks, can without much of a stretch be distinguished and found.

Effectively observing crude materials, work in process, and completed designer can help organizations in keeping up a lean assembling framework and a cost preservationist organization. At the point when their providers execute this framework, a constant flow of value, on-time materials will stream into the plant and onto the assembling floor. This decreases stock, opens up extra space revenue driven making tasks, and lessens the outstanding burden of the workers. With more organizations requiring JIT (just-in-time) conveyances, this is one technique it very well may be cultivated. Six Sigma programs when executed by client and provider to meet their data and material stream can spare each impressive cost and improve benefits for both including the client. Playing out a Kaizen may likewise be considered and can be fruitful when very much planned to streamline produce. Make certain before doing a Kaizen that the framework will really be improved not simply the mechanical production system fixed.

BENCHMARKING

Building up and utilizing benchmarks in a Six Sigma or any quality program is required to know the condition of the procedure or activity at time zero and the amount of an improvement has been accomplished both during, and at the decision, of a program. The utilization of the milestone display chart will help with keeping a program on plan in addition to outwardly show plant staff their association in the improvement procedure.

Most Six Sigma improvement programs require cooperations with different divisions. These obvious diagrams would then be able to be a bit of leeway to alarm and guarantee materials, equipments, and services are prepared and accessible when required to proceed with the improvement procedure. At that point when the services are set up, the benchmark reference is utilized as a manual for check whether the objective was cultivated. Benchmarks can be utilized as focuses of achieved all through the program. Objectives can be assessed during the program with work plans raised or brought down contingent upon the outcomes accomplished to date.

Visual pointers show the aftereffects of the improvement program. They are followed after a benchmark beginning stage is resolved to check whether the projects objectives are being accomplished. Markers in a procedure will show noticeably what direction the procedure is moving, is it stable, and in charge. These pointers can be plotted on a control diagram to noticeable show program progress and may manage the group to consider and assess other key factors if the pattern is off course. These markers must be continually assessed for importance in genuine foreseeing the result of the program. At the point when a variable change doesn't affect a marker, it might diminish in significance in the assessment procedure. Utilize the markers to keep the procedure enhancement for course for an effective end.

In business upgrades, markers may not be as self-evident. Posing inquiry of faculty utilizing the improved procedure might be a decent pointer. Reactions, for example, "for what reason wasn't this done previously", "it truly spares me a few repetitive advances I needed to do previously", and so on and furthermore "negative criticism". Remarks, for example, "I discover this to troublesome" or "the data required is rarely accessible or on schedule", and so on., "another person does likewise section in another division", and so on, can be a constructive impact when investigated for development.

APPLYING SIX SIGMA TOOLS FOR CONTINUED IMPROVEMENT

The entirety of the Six Sigma quality devices and measurements (statistical process control, graphing, and analysis) can be included into the organization's offices, administrations or service, and assembling regions. The familiar maxim KISS (keep it simple stupid) can be extended to KISS OFF (keep it scientific, simple, ordered, fundamental, and fun). Quality can be fun when you are attempting to forestall future problems even in organizationsthat oppose change. It is essential to recollect what the letters of the saying represent as keep it.

Scientific: refers to, utilizing the quality control measurements that are important to screen the process.

Simple: utilize Standard and handily comprehended measurements to accumulate the ideal information with process control graphs with determined UCL and LCL with at least five information focuses at set interims. These focuses then diminished to a solitary plotting point will for the most part be illustrative of recording the control of a progressing procedure inside sensible control. Be that as it may, as the procedure approaches Six Sigma, singular readings will turn out to be increasingly significant when taken at recommended, planned internals.

Ordered: implies the information was assembled in a technique simple to acquire, record, and use. The information can be electronically gotten over a foreordained time or cycle period that will show the repeatability of the procedure or framework under investigation.

Key, implies identifying with the quality or assembling procedure or program under examination. Assemble just the information that is required to show the procedure control focuses and the factors that control the activity.

Fun, implies only that. The activity must be made to be charming and all work force who have a stake in the activity ready to grant their own capacities into the program. They possess the procedure and program and need to make it a triumph. Make it a success win program for the administrators, representatives, the executives and corporate administration. Avoid dangers of what will occur if that it doesn't work. Be certain so innovative and open reasoning will consistently win. The carrot not the club as an excessive number of the executive's faculty from the old school like to utilize.

These information focuses are normally accumulated as individual readings, added, arrived at the midpoint of, and plotted as a procedure point on the control graph. Other metric information is likewise produced in the product program, standard deviation, run, and so on., which is utilized to show the change of control around the mean inside the procedure.

TYPES OF TESTING: APPRAISAL, CONFIRMATION AND CHARACTERIZATION

There are three kinds of testing which must be considered for appropriation to precisely track and control the process. Additionally, recall every client have their own degree of adequate item quality they will use in choosing a provider of their items. They will need what they contracted for and client needs will differ from exact medicinal and electronic items to less exact items as plastic rubbish holders and disposable drinking cups.

APPRAISAL TESTING

This form of testing decides how well an item addresses the client's issues for commonly structure, fit, and capacity. This is the strategy utilized for testing when fabricating process factors are obscure and should be set up to make adequate items. At the point when the items attributes fulfill the client's desires and particulars it is regarded acceptable. It is then discharged to the commercial center paying little heed to the control prerequisites of the assembling procedure used to deliver the item. As the organization producing process moves to Six Sigma to lessen absconds, improve yield, and diminish cost, examination testing ought to be supplanted with affirmation and portraying testing. These types of testing move from, "Is the item fitting in with particulars?" to "Is the assembling procedure making the item change?"

CONFIRMATION TESTING

This testing strategy decides whether there are changes simultaneously. It is utilized when manufacturing variables are known and the procedure is in statistical process control. This is when "Ongoing" testing of item is basic to yield quality. Item dimensional information and insights are assembled as quickly as time permits with the goal that procedure variable modifications can be made "Real Time" control.

Each process will affect the item. Check when the item will arrive at balance or when stable before taking an estimation. Since every single plastic item require a particular measure of time to even out to their last measurements, it was a propensity to "prejudge", the measure of post shape shrinkage. This is the place the last measurements would stabilizer after the part was simply expelled from the device in a hot unsteady (despite everything contracting) item condition. A strategy for deciding, hot as shaped measurements versus cold after ordinarily a 24 hour chill off period, were created to accomplish an expected material shrinkage rate to meet last part balanced out measurements.

Parts can be apportioned just of the instrument by utilizing go/no go gages or installations dependent on hot measurements that on chill off are known to accomplish explicit measurements after a foreordained timeframe and will meet the client's prerequisites. These measurements can be utilized to evaluate variable modifications "Continuously". This requires more preplanning and could possibly be required relying upon the client's details. I offer this as thought when at first modifying the assembling procedure to get it into satisfactory item control for deformity decrease toward the beginning of production. By utilizing the items hot measurements, a gifted expert can modify the procedure "Progressively" when they recognize what the items last measurements will be after chilled off.

At that point as the assembling procedure improves and stays in process control, item testing and estimation turns out to be less basic. Control of the procedure factors guarantees the items factors stay in charge and part to-parcel repeatability and attributes have consistency. Checking and controlling assembling factors "Progressively" will in the end lead to affirming item factors are accomplished. This testing alongside process information will reaffirm nothing unanticipated has happened in the assembling procedure.

CHARACTERIZATION TESTING

This testing is utilized to portray the impacts of procedure changes on a procedure or item. This is the most exact type of testing which gauges the littlest changes in a control variable.

Characterization test looks at an assembling procedure by describing the impacts on an item for a known arrangement of process factors, and any progressions happening all the while. This testing technique expect something in the process has changed. This requires adequate testing to portray the procedure factors that changed the item and to decide it's close to term consequences for the item.

Characterization testing will require progressively stringent variable examination utilizing quality methodology to gather the more inconspicuous variable changes to achieve a higher level of process exactness. This will include more example estimations utilizing progressively explicit and more prominent precision estimating instruments. Continuously utilize exceptionally prepared controllers and experts to guarantee the information gathered is as exact as could reasonably be expected. Utilize the most explicit inspecting philosophies to get the most elevated precision in your information as the way to Success. In a develop fabricating process-Six Sigmatesting has two necessities; affirmation and portrayal.

IMPLEMENTING THE SIX SIGMA IMPROVEMENT PROGRAM

Procedure 1. Committed Management Leadership

The leaders for actualizing Six Sigma need the capacity to settle on proficient and extreme choices influencing the future accomplishment of their business. Being a leader isn't just assigning, yet additionally, appointing duty to other who show commitment, capable, and learned leaders that have the "edge", to lead the Six Sigma program forward. This incorporates driving the Six Sigma ventures and showing their different directors these equivalent hands-on strategies.

Procedure 2. Integrating Using Existing Initiatives, Business Strategy and Key Performance Measures

The management incorporates Six Sigma philosophy into all aspects of the organization utilizing Six Sigma techniques to intensify set up strategies, business systems, and execution measurements. Incorporating Six Sigma enhancements techniques at the specialty unit level while supplementing the organization's long-haul objectives is key for progress. This is typically lead by a senior supervisory group concentrating on driving home its significance to every one of their workers.

Procedure 3. Framework for Process Thinking

Before any quantitative analysis event can start, you should recognize what frameworks are set up and being utilized to help you in meeting your client prerequisites. Essentially, build up a benchmark for enhancements. To do this you should thoroughly delineate existing business procedures to create and dissect quantitatively, your presentation. Utilizing QFD numerous client and provider inquiries on framework prerequisites can be characterized. The framework must realize what the client requires for their utilization in affirming the quality required is achievable from your organization.

Six Sigma is reducing the information and data gap between CCR's (Critical Customer Requirement) and your business and assembling capacity that is named "process sigma." The separation between your ability and CCR's is utilized to organize your Six Sigma endeavors. The smaller the gap, the closer you are to meeting reliably your CCR's.

In this manner, when your boss at first chooses a program, talk about it with them, to guarantee the program isn't a segregated venture with low client significance. Be certain a program can turn into a piece of an organized system of enhancements, as these will understand a quicker pace of complete achievement. These projects are progressively engaged and proficient in light of the fact that improvement in one will interpret through every other program to start later. They center consideration around item output and market request as opposed to depending on a person's instinct.

Procedure 4. Disciplined Gathering of Customer and Market Intelligence

Six Sigma will help the organization in remaining in direct contact with their client's needs, existing level of consumer satisfaction, and increase them Six Sigma Improvements in Business dedication in being a favored provider of their items. Cooperation of suppliers and client key contacts is strengthened with communication, inter-company. This is at all levels. Connections are created which are critical to learning consumer loyalty at all levels. Client information can help with knowing at-regularly updated where the market is going.

Regularly some CCR data may not generally be given, not as a unintended mystery, yet frequently not understood at the time the QFD is led. New prerequisites can happen at whenever and ideally are promptly transmitted to the provider. They ought to be transmitted as an ECO (designing change request) utilizing an ECR (building change demand) structure to be recognized with any refreshed drawings and guidelines.

This is utilized to guarantee the provider has total comprehension of the solicitation. Duty regarding any WIP (work in process) must be resolved and if the change can be made for finished units. If not, renegotiations must be cultivated before a status is accomplished for these products. A solicitation at a cost decrease can likewise be transmitted dependent on rivalry dangers to you or your client. This requires a shut circle insight social occasion and data move procedure to be set up to accumulate client and market information. This information should then be converted into hard estimations that can be broke down normally and contrasted with business yield procedures and transmitted to the provider.

Procedure 5. Projects Must Produce Real Savings and Revenues

Restoring a positive income from a Six Sigma program is the objective. In the past other quality improvements programs did not have a genuine observing of income in any event, when fruitful. Therefore, numerous prior quality projects, for example, TQM, zero imperfections, quality circles, and so forth., were not proceeded as Six Sigma Improvements in Business outcomes on the reality, which made a difference to the executives, was not constantly accessible or archived. Again, and again the main expense of value data was the pay numbers for the division, improve, scrap, returns and guarantee substitution things. Thus, many were not proceeded as results on the primary concern were not precisely followed, archived and detailed. Lessening cost of value requires characterized programs with staff alloted errands, finishing information, observing with results detailed week after week to the executives for examination bolster when required. Six Sigma extends new to organization the executives may demand transient compensation that is in strife to Procedure 3, long haul with recompense improving a chain of distinguished, progressive undertakings.

This is an issue for some, organizations following their expense of value even before beginning Six Sigma programs. The following of their Six Sigma work force is achievable. Yet, archiving the genuine expenses of value without extraordinary thought of what information is to be really gathered is extremely troublesome. The expenses are typically separated in Prevention,

Appraisal, and Warranty. The obligation is on the quality staff to work with their controller to create charge codes for depicting the sort of activity performed and precisely recording these expenses. This is significant with the goal that charges for time and material will be accurately recognized for the class of value anticipation work they are performing.

Building up an expense of value pattern starts before any program is begun so results can be observed. Quality issues start with poor generation estimate arranging and with requesting an inappropriate material that defers the production of a program. Getting an inappropriate confirmation or investigation data is a quality issue and endeavors must be made to guarantee all related quality cost regions are recognized and charged so a precise gauge and future quality expenses are created for the organization's actual expense of value program.

Procedure 6. Reward the Achievers

Organizations who reward accomplishment at all degrees of their organization dependent on accomplishments, are likewise compensated by representatives who endeavor to accomplish the objectives of the organization. Six Sigma offers these acknowledgment difficulties to all who are chosen for the program. A few organizations have actualized new acknowledgment programs for Six Sigma experts and officials who have overseen six sigma effective projects in their areas of expertise.

PROFITING FROM PREVENTIVE MAINTENANCE

Preventive upkeep implies being proactive to forestall hardware disappointment and framework issues. Complexity this way to deal with symptomatic or restorative support, which is performed to address an effectively existing issue. In the event that you have and take care of a vehicle, you may comprehend the idea of preventive upkeep: you don't replace your oil in light of an issue circumstance – you do it before things turn out badly, so your motor endures longer and you dodge vehicle inconveniences not far off. Preventive support is a calendar of arranged upkeep activities focused on the counteraction of breakdowns and disappointments. Forestalling the disappointment of hardware before it really happens is the essential objective. Preventive upkeep is intended to protect and upgrade gear dependability by supplanting worn segments before they fizzle and exercises incorporate hardware checks, incomplete or complete updates at determined periods, oil changes, grease, etc. In addition,workers can record gear decay so they know to supplant or fix worn parts before they cause framework disappointment. Later mechanical advances in instruments for investigation and analysis have empowered considerably progressively precise and viable gear upkeep.

A perfect preventive support program forestalls all gear disappointment before it happens. For instance, in an air terminal, preventive support might be set up in basic help regions, for example, elevators, lighting and airplane spans. Likewise with all anticipation movement, a few people consider preventive to be as unduly expensive. This rationale directs that customary booked personal time and support is more expensive than working hardware until fix is totally vital – and likely could be valid for certain segments. Long haul advantages and investment funds related with preventive upkeep, in any case, likewise should be considered.

Without preventive support, for instance, costs for lost help time from unscheduled hardware breakdown will be brought about, something that would get evident through OEE measures. Likewise, preventive support brings about investment funds by expanding the administration life of powerful frameworks. Long haul advantages of preventive upkeep include: Improved framework unwavering quality. Diminished expense of substitution. Diminished framework personal time. Better extras stock administration. You can't generally keep things from turning out badly or hardware from fizzling. However, when they do, your capacity to bounce back from issues rapidly is critical.

SPREADING THE LOAD

Keeping things adjusted and level methods your process streams are smoother and your general handling times quicker. Be that as it may, be cautioned – this circumstance isn't anything but difficult to accomplish, either at work or on your way there! Consider variable speed restrains on motorways, which expect to keep up a consistent, ceaseless progression of traffic, empowering us to all continue moving and stay away from stops and starts during occupied periods. Tragically, a few drivers consistently accelerate between the speed cameras, possibly to brake hard when they find a good pace one, a methodology that makes braking and delay down the street. In the work environment, you have to attempt to keep away from pinnacles and troughs in movement, if you can. The monthor quarter-end cycles in numerous associations feature the challenges of pinnacles. Actioning money related compromises, for instance, on an every day or week by week premise might be conceivable, in this way staying away from the month to month or quarterly pinnacle of movement. You have to decide if a chance to change frequencies exists in your organization.

CARRYING OUT WORK IN A STANDARD WAY

Now and then, the initial phase in forestalling issues and revamp is concurring on a standard procedure. Defining a standard procedure gives you genuine gains effectively and prompts steadiness and consistency all the while. As a matter of fact, you can't generally start to improve a procedure until you institutionalize it.

Following institutionalization, you have a veritable opportunity to settle the procedure and brief further upgrades. Institutionalizing the 'one most ideal method for' how the work completes is vital, yet in a culture of ceaseless improvement you may discover better approaches to take every necessary step that become the upgraded 'one most ideal way', until further improvement happens. Obviously, if deserts happen, your first inquiry should be, 'Has the standard procedure been followed?' If it has, at that point the procedure should be improved.

Right now of consistent improvement, fuelled and bolstered by Lean Six Sigma, you have to continue improving your procedure, empowering thoughts from the individuals working inside it. As you become progressively certain about applying the Lean Six Sigma standards, so you'll perceive that there's no closure to the way toward improving procedures!

CHAPTER SEVEN: ANALYSING WHAT'S AFFECTING BUSINESS PERFORMANCE

Regardless of whether you deal with a day-today activity or are engaged with a DMAIC (Define, Measure, Analyze, Improve and Control) improvement venture, you have to comprehend what factors can influence performance, particularly in the event that you experience issues in meeting your clients' necessities. There is prologue to a determination of tools and processes to assist you with recognizing the 'guilty parties'. How and how well the work gets done is centered around the procedure and the information.

UNEARTHING THE USUAL SUSPECTS

Individuals regularly form a hasty opinion about the potential reasons for issues. In numerous organizations, managers appear to 'know' without a doubt what the causes are; generally, in any case, an entire scope of suspects impact execution and influence your capacity to meet clients' CTQs (Critical To Quality) – yet risks are just an essential few are really 'blameworthy'.

GENERATING YOUR LIST OF SUSPECTS

In order to find the part which is guilty, you produce a rundown of potential causes, look at every conceivable reason and bit by bit, thin down the rundown. Right now, take a look at the strategies accessible to assist you with uncovering the suspects.

CREATING A CAUSE AND EFFECT DIAGRAM

The fishbone, or which is also known as 'cause and effect', chart was created by Dr. Ishikawa and gives a valuable method for gathering and exhibiting thoughts from a what has been brainstormed.

The head of the fish contains an inquiry that portrays the impact you are exploring (ensure you pick a barely engaged inquiry or you'll wind up with a whalebone!). For instance, you may solicit, 'What are the potential reasons for delays in conveying client requests?' or 'For what reason are there such a large number of blunders in our solicitations?' You can gather the conceivable brainstormed and causes under whatever headings you pick. For instance, the conventional headings of People, Equipment, Method, Materials and

Environment, can be utilized. You may discover these headings valuable in provoking thoughts during the brainstorming act., however know that they can likewise restrain progressively on lateral reasoning. The group concocts their thoughts on the potential causes, composing the thoughts on clingy notes with the goal that you can move them around effectively during the ensuing arranging process.

Spot your significant reason headings on the left-hand side of the graph, framing the fundamental 'bones' of the fish. The conceptualized thoughts (the potential root cause) structure the littler bones. For every conceivable reason, pose the inquiry 'For what reason do we think this a potential reason?' and rundown the reactions as littler bones falling off the fundamental driver. You may need to ask 'Why?' a few times to distinguish the plausible explanation, however you may in any case need to approve this with information. Utilize an interrelationship graph straightaway, to assist you with concentrating on the correct Xs (or info factors). Utilizing an interrelationship chart (ID) causes you recognize the key drivers behind the impact you're exploring in your fishbone graph.

INVESTIGATING THE SUSPECTS AND GETTING THE FACTS

Business managing or overseeing by reality is crucial, so approving the potential causes featured by your interrelationship outline is the following stage. Each one of those potential causes are honest until demonstrated liable. To approve your causes, you may need to watch the procedure and go to the Gemba (where the work completes or look at the information to see whether they validate your intuitions. You'll most likely need to gather some extra information to do this.

In Lean Six Sigma talk, the output measures are Y data, and the outcomes here are impacted by the upstream X factors. Xs and Ys are in reality noble motivation and impact. Separately and in a collective manner, the different Xs impact your presentation in meeting the client CTQs, the Y factors. Some of the time, Xs are alluded to as 'free factors' and Ys as 'needy factors'. Unmistakably, the Y results rely upon you dealing with the Xs cautiously. A SIPOC chart gives a aperfect structure to assist you with considering all your procedure measures and now you have to arrange a lot of X measures, on the off chance that you don't as of now have them. A scope of X factors will be coming into your procedure – the 'input factors'. These info factors influence the presentation of the Ys, and may incorporate the volume of exercises, for instance the number and sort of new requests. These info factors may well concern the exhibition of your providers, as well, maybe as far as the degree of exactness, culmination and practicality of the different things being sent to you. The data sources may be from clients or providers, yet in any case, they'll sway on how you perform. How frequently do you have to return for missing data or more clear directions, for instance? A scope of X factors will exist in the process itself – the 'inprocess factors'. Here, your arrangement flowchart or value stream guide can assist you with featuring the potential Xs, including movement and process durations, levels of adjust, the accessibility of individuals or machine personal time, for instance. Once more, these Xs will influence your presentation. As you distinguish the X estimates you need, so you're builan equalization of measures to assist you with dealing with your procedure. You are probably going to find that the SIPOC and organization flowchart are particularly useful here.

PROVING YOUR POINT

At the point when you think you know the reason for the problem in your procedure, you may need to give some proof to back it up. For instance, your supervisor may think he/she knows the appropriate response, however you may discover something other than what's expected as the aftereffect of your cautious examination of the realities. You can utilize a straightforward grid to show how the different bits of proof match against the suspects. This grid is once in a while alluded to as legitimate reason testing, where you condense the potential reasons for the issue, and show whether the different proof you've assembled from your procedure and information investigation intelligently coordinates the suspects.

Utilizing a Scatter diagram (in some cases alluded to as a Scatter plot) can assist you with fortifying your case. A dissipate outline encourages you distinguish whether a potential relationship or connection exists between two factors and empowers you to give an incentive to and measure that relationship. The factors are the circumstances and logical results – X and Y. You can utilize this technique to confirm potential underlying drivers of an issue or, for instance, to approve the connection between your information and in-process measures against your yield measures. If your presumed cause (X) is genuine, at that point any adjustments in X produce an adjustment in the impact (Y). Do be cautious, in any case, as correlation doesn't generally infer causation, and you have to utilize good judgment to make your determinations.

The dependent variable Y is constantly plotted on the vertical pivot, that of the independent X variable is plotted on the horizontal axis. The information is plotted in pair format. So, when X = 'this value', Y = 'that value'.

SEEING THE POINT

Basically, observing the picture might be sufficient to show that you have or haven't found the underlying cause of your problem, yet to fortify your case you can put an incentive on the connection between the factors by figuring the correlation coefficient, or r value. This value measures the connection between the X and the Y – it discloses to you the quality of the relationship, be it positive or negative, regarding the measure of variation the X is causing in the Y results. In a superbly positive connection, r = +1. In an impeccably negative connection, r = – 1. Normally the relationship coefficient is short of what one, as the plausibility of just a single X influencing the presentation of the Y is improbable; by and large, a few will be obvious and it's presumable you will have decided the correlation coefficient value for each of these. Very likely, be that as it may, one X will cause the most variety.

The connection coefficient becomes clearer with somewhat more maths (don't be worried – some softwares, for example, Excel, JMP or Minitab can do it for you). The value r2 (the coefficient of determination) shows the level of variation in Y clarified by the impact of X. For instance, if r = 0.7, the variable is causing 49 percent of the variety in Y; if r = 0.8, the worth increments to 64 percent. In both of these conditions, you appear to have discovered the significant cause of the issue as these qualities are especially high, particularly looking at that as various different Xs are additionally impacting the Y results. With a lower esteem, for instance where r = 0.2 or 0.3, the effect is generally little, representing 4 percent and 9 percent, separately.

At the point when only one X is included, this figuring is known as basic linear regression. Different regression stretches out the procedure to cover a few Xs, as designs of analyses, yet these increasingly included statistical techniques are well advanced. Linear regression empowers you to make forecasts for the estimation of Y with various estimations of X, however recall that the straight line probably won't proceed until the end of time. As showed before, a limit may exist where things change significantly. Forsake rate in a call community is a genuine case of an edge point existing where: guests may be set up to hold tight the line for a sensible time, however at one point they become furious and hammer the telephone down.

Scatter diagrams are anything but difficult to deliver utilizing software, for example, JMP, Excel or Minitab. In any case, know about a portion of the regular mistakes and traps related with them, for example, stirring up the X and Y factors and tomahawks or making the presumption that connection infers causation. Relationship doesn't generally infer causation, and you have to

utilize sound judgment to make your inferences. Understanding the different Xs influencing the presentation of your procedure is significant. When you've recognized your Xs, you can guarantee the correct measures are set up and can move in the direction of making steady and unsurprising execution.

ASSESSING YOUR EFFECTIVENESS

A few 'Lean measures' are accessible to assist you with getting the required performance and the rate of improvement which is needed ze of progress required, including Takt time and by and large procedure viability and Overall Equipment Effectiveness.

Taking Takt time into account

Takt time reveals to you how rapidly you have to action things corresponding to client request. Takt is German for an exact interim of time, for example, a melodic meter. It fills in as the cadence or beat of the procedure – the recurrence at which an item or service must be finished so as to address client issues. The formula for Takt time is the accessible production time divided by the client request: The accessible time is free of what number of assets are accessible. It speaks to the quantity of working hours in the day or move. For instance, if a gadget manufacturing plant works 480 minutes out of every day and clients request 100 gadgets for each day, Takt time is 288 seconds, or 4.80 minutes. In the event that request is for 240 gadgets, the Takt time would be two minutes. Additionally, if clients need two new items for each month, Takt time is two weeks.

Perceiving the impact of revamp is significant, in light of the fact that it viably lessens the Takt time in direct extent. Along these lines, envision that in the model, a 10 percent blunder rate exists in the principal pass yield of the work, however this is gotten and amended. Basically, this 'builds' the quantity of client demands from 100 to 110, the 'accessible' minutes are unaltered at 480, yet the effect on Takt time is to adequately make it shorter, at 4.36 minutes. Takt time will be successfully shorter still on the off chance that we have secondpass adjustments to manage! In this way, the real Takt time may be 480, however the improve implies you have less time than that practically speaking.

Obviously, a significant relationship exists between Takt time, process duration and activity time. If the Takt time is not exactly the process duration you have a problem, which must be handled quickly, preferably utilizing DMAIC. Evacuating waste likely could be a piece of the arrangement; forestalling it in any case may be another. When Takt time rises to process duration 'immaculate stream' exists, however again and again the stream isn't adjusted. This circumstance can cause bottlenecks that upset your capacity to satisfy client need.

CONSIDERING OVERALL PROCESS AND EQUIPMENT EFFECTIVENESS

In breaking down your presentation, you may likewise need to set up some extra measures, for example, Overall Process Effectiveness (OPE) in value-based processes and Overall Process Effectiveness (OEE) in assembling. We use OPE and OEE to quantify and comprehend the presentation and adequacy of gear or procedures. Every one of these outline measures has three parts: accessibility, execution and quality.

The accessibility rate estimates losses with downtime from failure of equipment and adjustments as a percentage of the defined and booked time.

The exhibition rate estimates working operating speed losses – running at speeds lower than configuration speed and stoppages going on for brief periods as concurred.

The quality rate communicates misfortunes coming about because of scrap and improve as a level of absolute parts run.

These components are multiplied together, where OEE = Availability × Performance × Quality. Along these lines, with Availability at 90 percent, Performance at 95 percent and Quality at 99 percent, OEE = 0.90 × 0.95 × 0.99 = 84.6 percent. In service organizations, or for value-based procedures, OPE will in general be utilized. Here, you take the accompanying three components, again increasing them together to decide the OPE: A = accessibility of gear P = profitability Q = quality rate Take a gander at Lean for Dummies by Natalie J. Sayer and Bruce Williams (Wiley) for progressively point by point data about the OEE and OPE.

CONCLUSION: AVOIDING DISCREPANCIES

The vast majority of us need to do the correct things right. Process analysis is an extraordinary instrument to give us what we're doing and assist us with addressing the inquiries 'Why?' and 'Are we doing this progression accurately?' indeed, you have four choices:

Making the best choice right – the vast majority need to do this. Serving incredible nourishment and giving first rate services in a beautiful café is a model.

Making the best decision wrong – apply the tools to fix the issue. Envision incredible help and a delightful eatery however terrible nourishment. Tune in to the voice of the client, perceive that the low quality of the nourishment is the key driver of client disappointment and handle the root cause of the issue. That is, you examine the procedure, find the basic components basic the reasons for the issue and understand those. Frequently issues can be settled essentially; right now, by utilizing less salt.

Doing an inappropriate thing right – this is non-value adding. To proceed with the model, you focus on making the eatery look far and away superior yet at the same time serve dreadful nourishment. That is, you don't discover what the genuine client prerequisites are, hop to an inappropriate arrangement and go through superfluous cash.

. Doing an inappropriate thing incorrectly – attempting to get this privilege is inconsequential. For instance, going through loads of cash restyling the café when clients really preferred the prior style. A definitive peril is commencing a Lean Six Sigma venture to fix the circumstance in choice 4 above – and as yet winding up doing an inappropriate thing!

OVERTRAINING

Unmistakably, getting trained up in Lean Six Sigma is significant and an all-around considered training plan needs to form some portion of the general deployment program. Training works best when it's conveyed 'without a moment to spare' and at the correct level. In the good 'ol days, a few organizations embraced extensive, huge scale executions of Six Sigma and 'constrained' several individuals onto superfluous 20day Black Belt training, which brought about putting a significant number of them off the entire methodology.

An association simply beginning to utilize Lean Six Sigma will be loaded with various opportunities for process improvement that can be handled utilizing the devices learned on a decent establishment. In a perfect world, this six-day preparing can be part into three littler modules of two days each, folded over a genuine venture being done to guarantee the preparation is conveyed at the correct level and at the ideal time to fit into the life of the task.

THANKS FOR READING!!!